DR. KRISTY SINGER-MACNAIR

Untamable

How to Step Out of the Box and Let Yourself Fly

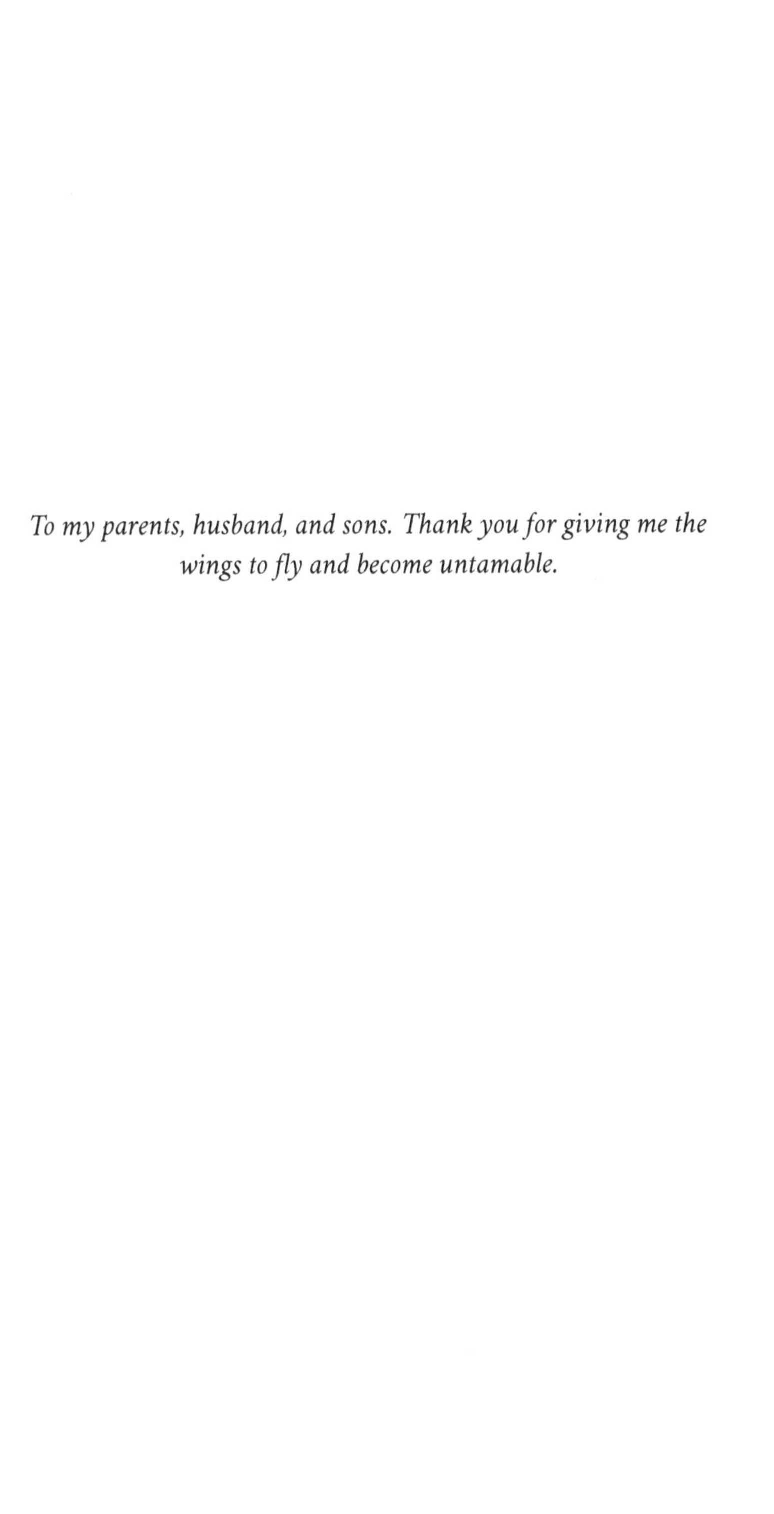

To my parents, husband, and sons. Thank you for giving me the wings to fly and become untamable.

Contents

When it comes to spirit, nature held nothing back with my mother, Dr. Kristy Singer. She is a person whose motivations hover above those of her contemporaries. Where there are questions to be asked, she not only leads the way with inquiry, but she also supplies answers. I have never seen her fazed by the size of a goal, for she revels in pushing envelopes and exceeding reasonable expectations. If life is a mountain, she isn't the mountaineer striving for the top. She is the puma that traverses the complexities of the range, day in and day out studying the intricacies of the landscape—unscripted and certainly untamable.

As you will shortly discover in the pages you presently hold, her life has been dedicated to the art of learning. She seamlessly toggles between educator and student. These are roles which she fills naturally. She is at her best when creating an environment that fosters fertility of mind. Never has she dismissed an opportunity to inspire the growth of those around her. What you'll find in *Untamable* is not only the story of a woman who lived up to that descriptor, but also one who has, for decades, inspired people around her to do the same.

I feel this book was written specifically to me. It serves as a portal to the crossroads of a time and a state of mind I have never had access to. Part memoir, part self-help, *Untamable* is truly a deeply personal and one-of-a-kind book. I know I will be returning to it for years to come when I need that door opened—to remind myself of who my mom truly is.

-Hunter MacNair, February 2023

Introduction

I'll bet anything that at some point, if not constantly, you've felt like other people were trying to tame you. Maybe someone shushed you when you tried to speak, cut you off when you started to state your opinion, or questioned your dreams. That happened to all of us when we were kids, but many of us feel that even as adults, someone is trying to tame us.

By tapping into your untamable nature and making positive changes, you can manage your own life instead of being contained or controlled by what others think. I've found life is more fulfilling when I release my powerful intuition to come through to help solve my problems.

When I was held back from those natural tendencies in my job, I felt tamed. I was only doing cookie-cutter work, which didn't serve my students or me. I'm much more creative now. In my position as a diagnostician in the field of special education, when I come up with reports and treatment ideas, I trust my intuition and look for diverse ways to help my students.

In my personal life, I've honed my communication skills to state my opinion while still being friendly, which has gone a long way with my family and friends. Being untamed opens other avenues to developing solid relationships. My search for love and the number of years of marriage to my wonderful husband is proof. If you are looking for a mate, this book will inspire you to be with someone who won't try to tame you but one who will help you transform into your true self.

Being untamable is a journey, not a destination. It's a process that has continued to open me to different views, both personally and professionally.

Nothing is as powerful as your authentic self. Trust yourself, and experiment with different ways to deal with situations in your personal and professional life.

What I hope you take away from my story is to unleash your own untamable nature.

I love hearing about the impact I've had on my students: helping them communicate appropriately, so they can freely make their needs and desires known, as well as having a voice.

That's my contribution, and I know you have one to make, too.

Tamed

So often, being tamed is something we're only fully aware of once we have the wisdom of hindsight.

In my case, my wise retrospection took me back to Modesto, California. George Lucas, born in Modesto in 1944, described it as a "Norman Rockwell town." The name means modest, and it seemed like an innocent place to live. I know because I was born there in 1949, five years after George Lucas.

This middle-class town in the scenic San Joaquin Valley used to be, and still remains, heavily agricultural with ranches, farmlands, factories for canning fruits, and almond orchards.

Baseball was a favorite pastime there, going back to 1872, when Modesto formed a community team that, in the 1890s, became the Modesto Reds—an independent minor league. Theater, dancing, and music were also popular with Modestans.

In 1904, Modesto's population doubled with the addition of a canal system to irrigate farmers' fields. That wasn't the only time the population boomed. My hometown had an explosion of growth. Following the post-World War II baby boom, a time during which I was born, the city had to build twelve new schools in seven years. That brings us to the 1950s and my childhood.

By the time I was born, Modesto had golf courses, baseball fields, and tennis courts, both community and private. My parents and twin sister, Kathy, were in a league at the bowling alley. We were involved in a lot of activities, and my parents exposed us to new experiences and types of entertainment, including cultural ones, as Modesto became home to the arts and music world.

A popular activity for teenagers of the time was "dragging 10th," which meant cruising downtown 10th Street. Of course, we had drive-ins, like in the movie *American Graffiti*, with the waitresses on roller skates bringing trays of hamburgers, fries, and milkshakes to our car window.

* * *

My mother and father were wonderful parents who were well known, liked, and respected in Modesto.

My mom, Sarah Louise Ramey, was born in Tennessee in 1924 and had three sisters. As a strong, independent, intelligent, and elegant woman, as well as a perfect "homemaker," she was a significant role model throughout my life. Mom approached situations with practicality and foresight and made good decisions for our family. In addition, she exuded charm and grace with people. My mother stayed home with us until my twin sister and I started junior high. When we'd arrive home from school, she'd prepare a beautiful dinner for our family. She kept a nice house, always clean and organized.

My dad, Donald Clarence Singer, was born in Nebraska in 1920 and had eleven siblings. He was a well-rounded child and later worked for his father's business. They faced trials and tribulations, losing family members to illness, accidents, and World War II. Dad served as a Marine during the war. Our parents wanted us to learn more about the Marines. When I was a young adult, we attended a reunion in Colorado and visited all the sites to better understand what my dad experienced while in the service during World War II.

Like Mom, Dad was intelligent, loving, and compassionate. He enjoyed learning something new every day, a trait I share with him.

I had another sister, Donna, who was three years older than my twin sister and me.

I distinctly remember a picture of three girls with perfect bangs and blond locks curled tightly and adorned with bows. Our family was an excellent unit that did all the right things and appeared to be "ideal."

My sister Kathy and I were almost viewed as one person—symbiotic. We were both always invited to the same birthday parties, though once in a while, we'd get invitations to different events, which felt weird to us.

My parents dressed us alike from a young age, and sometimes, our older sister also had a matching outfit. When we were little, my mother made most of our outfits by hand, along with the costumes for our ballet performances. She had a flair for sewing and certainly the talent of a fashion designer, but I also wanted store-bought prom dresses rather than my mom's designs.

The other side of having a twin is throughout our childhood, we were constantly compared. "She's this; you're that." It bothered me. I wanted to be me and not be pressured to conform to things my twin sister or others did.

A favorite family activity in the evening was playing board games together, which I still enjoy doing. I also looked forward to our family get-togethers. My dad was from a large family, and we had many relatives. I loved the family functions we attended at a lush, tree-shaded Modesto park because I connected with my immediate family and relatives. Situations, activities, and a sense of faith in my family carried me through the rest of my life. It was a wonderful childhood. It always seemed to me we were a happy family.

We lived in a house behind an elementary school that had a baseball field. For years, Dad sat in his chair by our fence breathing in the scent of fresh cut grass and listening to the crack of a baseball bat and laughing children as he watched the games.

Our home was also relatively near the train tracks. Central Pacific Railroad basically founded Modesto in 1870 by buying a square mile of land and selling lots. We could hear the chugging of the locomotives from our house. Later, those railroads were replaced by beautiful trails where people can now walk or ride a bike for miles, almost to the center of Modesto.

Every Sunday, our family went to the First United Methodist Church. Following the service, we would arrive home and have a Sunday dinner. Then, we discussed our plans for the coming week, so my mom could prepare anything she'd volunteered to cook or bake for our school.

In addition, my sisters and I were involved in Rainbow Girls, a young women's group that taught confidence, leadership, and citizenship. We also wore lovely dresses that met the dress code for the meetings.

Kathy and I were popular at school. In fact, we experienced jealousy from some of the other students because we were well-liked, dressed nicely, and had a great family. Within the large group of friends we had, Kathy was closer to some, I was better friends with others, and some overlapped. From a young age, we were socially active and enjoyed athletic activities such as hopscotch and tetherball. This continued throughout our high school years, except the activities evolved into competitive sports (track, gymnastics, basketball, baseball, dance, and more).

* * *

My parents were role models in the community. Dad taught me the importance of education, responsibility, family, moral values, and compassion. As an adult, I continued consulting my dad for his grounded advice for problem-solving situations. When my friends became teenagers, they consulted with him, which continued throughout their lives. And my mother was a perfectionist.

From that modeling, I insisted on perfection in myself, which brought on shyness and pressure to never say anything wrong. I always filtered what I said, afraid I might hurt someone's feelings, becoming "tamable" because I felt vulnerable about offering my own views and opinions. In addition, even though I loved to tease and joke, I feared people would laugh at me or think I was goofy. As a result, I was far more comfortable talking to others one-on-one rather than in group situations.

My mom would say things to other people like, "Oh, don't say that in front of Kristy," treating me as if I were fragile and innocent. That came from my mom's belief that I was this picture-book, naïve, model child.

While she wasn't trying to undermine me, my mother's projection led to my long-standing lack of confidence and difficulty stating my views and rights. I wanted to follow all the rules when interacting with others. That continued well into high school and lingered into my adult years.

As I got older, both of my sisters would say or do things that hurt my feelings.

I remember my sister, Donna, often said, "Oh, really?" mocking me sarcastically instead of engaging in a deeper conversation about matters. When I discussed my ideas or mentioned specific topics, I felt put down, primarily by Donna and occasionally by Kathy.

One time, when I came up with a creative answer to something, Kathy said, "Oh, you're just so stupid."

Occasionally, I felt pressure from my mom not to speak up by stating my opinions or questioning things instead of readily accepting them. Again, this is tied to pressure, within the home, to be perfect. I felt the need to be flawless in everything and do what people expected of me in all areas of my life. So, I accepted the role of the sweet little girl who did everything just right and who was relentlessly polite.

I remember having a similar experience in a group of friends, when one was teasing, "Oh, watch how easily Kristy laughs." It was so embarrassing to have him say that in front of the group, which contributed to my self-consciousness. I interpreted that as, *Oh no, I have to be careful, quiet down, and not try to expand my personality.*

However, by the end of elementary school, due to having a curious mind, I began asking loads of questions. My parents called me "Kristy Why." I was beginning to feel a sense of experimentation with more open communication.

If I could change anything about my childhood, I'd choose to be less sensitive to teasing or criticism from others and counter those remarks with my natural sense of humor. Or I would choose to accept that it's part of life and not let it bother me because that tendency created my shyness and reluctance to speak up for myself. These memories come to me even today. I'm haunted by how easily offended and embarrassed I became by various experiences.

But I am letting go, accepting my new purpose in life, and practicing effective communication skills, and I am more aware of different perspectives in my personal and professional life. I also encourage others to experience the freedom to explore those opportunities.

By meeting my parents' expectations of how I looked in the community, I tended to be the teacher's pet in class. I enjoyed getting good grades, being kind and respectful to peers and adults, and having a fun sense of humor. That continued throughout my life. Although I did well for myself, the unrealistic demand of always saying nice things led me to feel constrained as a child.

* * *

During the era I grew up—even to this day—there seems to be a difference in how people treat men versus women. Throughout history, women have had to work for equalization and to eradicate discrimination. Men have had more control over the world, holding positions of higher seniority and earning higher salaries in the workforce.

But something interested me. I noticed my mother seemed to have more power in our family. She was an independent woman. And my father aimed to create a feeling of independence in his daughters. I remember Dad teaching us karate because he wanted us to defend ourselves and feel more confident.

* * *

Approaching high school, I felt tamed in many ways. Kathy often told me what to do because she saw me learning to take less at face value. I was trying to pull away from that tamed feeling and began to fly with my wings.

I wanted to express my opinions around extended family and my parents' friends, but I didn't want to seem confrontational or bug people with beliefs I had that differed from theirs. I was extremely uncomfortable around opinionated men. I said what I thought they were expecting to hear and never voiced my experience. This applied to older men, teachers, and authority figures.

During that era, little girls were always good and did what they were expected to do. This meant not arguing with others or stating their own opinions. So, when people confronted me, I clammed up and sometimes walked away, instead of formulating my reasons or ideas, so they'd take another look at the situation.

When I attended the University of California in the late 1960s and early 1970s, women were noticed and respected more as equals. It was a time of enormous cultural and societal shifts for women, though not as much as it should have been. There was an emphasis on feeling free and thinking outside of the box.

I began offering my opinions and standing up for my rights, evolving from being tamed to being true to myself.

During that time, everyone talked about the movie and play *Hair*, which I saw in San Francisco and Southern California. Besides the scanty clothes, the play was about freedom and people voicing their views, which really impacted me, though I was shy about it.

I remember an experience after graduating when I attended an informational meeting about EST, where the self-help training program tried to influence people to sign up for their classes.

Erhard Seminars Training (EST) was an organization founded by Werner Erhard in 1971—The EST Standard Training. The training brought forth the ideas of transformation, personal responsibility, accountability, and possibility.

I observed a young couple who looked like they were expecting a child and seemed like they didn't have a lot of extra money. The EST people pressured them to pay a lot to sign up for their program. I reacted intensely but fairly. Standing in the crowded auditorium, I discussed other choices rather than convincing them this company wanted to get rich. Then I walked away.

I thought, *Okay. I said what I felt.* And I know my actions had an impact on other people who were in the auditorium.

Although it felt great to do that, I was, at that stage, compartmentalizing situations in which I could feel free and speak my mind.

I began working in the public school district in special education where we conducted individualized meetings for students entering the special education program, a process that required extensive paperwork. I presented information to support the families and to help with their educational decisions.

At the start of my career, when I began manifesting free thinking, I experienced uncomfortable confrontations with educational directors and administrators. They needed more time to accept other options.

So, I thought, *Well, I have to play by the rules and tame myself to meet expectations at school with principals and directors. But I can express myself freely in my personal life.*

Throughout my adult life, there were times when I wouldn't share my views and feelings or present out-of-the-box ideas, even though they were in my thoughts. I felt trapped, needing to be respected as an individual with unique ideas.

For example, there was a case where an administrator disagreed with my recommendation that a student should be enrolled in the department's services. I said, flat out, "I don't agree with this IEP," and refused to sign off on it.

As I matured into a less-rigid individual, it grew more difficult to work in an environment with specific guidelines and rules with no room for questioning. Rules are appropriate if they serve a purpose or a function. However, I needed help with practices that needed to be clarified.

I worked best with the school administrators who listened to my presented results. However, with administrators who were set in their ways, I dug in my heels and did what I was supposed to do. Still, I felt confined, cut off from my creativity, intuition, and passion to plan for a student's success.

I've been told by some administrators that I'm a creative speech pathologist. I prefer to review a student's regular program to see what I can create to help develop plans to support their communication skills and academic success. This approach has increased my students' success.

Looking back, I should have had more tact when I started to firmly state my opinions, to question things, and to make suggestions. Those feelings were so strong in me that I wanted to express them. But, with experience in using elegant communication skills, maturity, and observation of reactions to how I've said things, I've learned to phrase things in a more listener-friendly way while still feeling heard.

I've grown more unrestrained in my life and can state my opinions and stand up for my students' rights. An administrator I've been working with recently advocated this expressive, out-of-the-box approach in a professional setting. She recognized the benefit of exploring more options and information to structure treatment for a particular child's case.

Each year, I feel freer and more comfortable with my life's direction. I'm no longer the tamed little girl from Modesto.

Shaping the Self

My journey to becoming untamed was a gradual process. Beginning in middle school, I had inquisitive thoughts and urges to express my ideas and perspectives on many different topics. When I left home for college, my ideas developed and expanded.

How I decided to specialize in speech pathology was serendipitous. I was out with my mom and ran into an administrator in the Modesto City school system.

He asked, "What do you want to do?"

"I want to go into education," I said.

He advised, "There's a lot of educators out there. You might take a look at being a reading or speech specialist."

That resonated with me. I shadowed a speech pathologist at a public school to learn what she did and what the job involved. I watched her help young people who had significant needs with developing their communication skills. All of that added to my desire to get a degree in the field. I decided on speech pathology because I've always loved how people express themselves and communicate. Even if I didn't realize it at the time, I was also driven to help others learn how to become untamed.

When deciding on a college, I researched schools near the beach. I knew the University of California at Santa Barbara had a reputable speech and hearing pathology program. One of my parents' friends gave me pointers on writing my college admissions essay since that was a crucial piece of the application process. That, combined with my numerous extracurricular activities and good grades, increased my likelihood for admission to UCSB. As luck would have it, three of my close friends were also accepted to UCSB.

After living in a small, conservative town, attending UCSB was an eye-opening experience. Those were the days of psychedelic, counterculture, eco-conscious lifestyles, of doing our own thing. It was also a time of activism and the Civil Rights Movement. The Black Panthers and gay rights activists were deep in the fight for equality. The women's liberation movement was in full swing with Betty Freidan's *The Feminine Mystique.* Women were protesting to gain full gender equality in law and in practice and to end sexism, sexist exploitation, and oppression.

I remembered going to my first big concert, grooving to the

music, and watching people's reactions and interactions. It was all a huge contrast from how I, and other girls, had been raised in small towns like Modesto.

At the beginning of college, it was pretty evident my parents were trying to encourage or "control" whom I could and could not date. Most of the men I dated attended college, and they were intelligent "good boys."

I chafed at the intrusion and started dating a ski instructor, knowing he was not the type of person my parents would approve of according to their standards. His family was friendly but also not up to the level of my parent's expectations, and he wasn't enrolled in college.

I enjoyed my time with him and had a blast with him, feeling freer and going on camping trips together (which my parents weren't happy about). However, it became apparent that the relationship wasn't going anywhere, so that ended. In hindsight, I was probably making a statement to my parents and growing and becoming more varied in my interests and opportunities outside of my hometown.

In Santa Barbara, I met different types of men, which increased my interest in the diversity of people and their backgrounds. I enjoyed dating men who could introduce me to fresh ideas about many topics. I probably wasn't as liberal as many of them, but for me, liberal meant being able to discuss my thoughts. We'd go to the plaza at the university, near the fountains, where people played music, danced, and had beach parties. These experiences solidified my interest in living near a beach town.

I learned a lot about myself from developing friendships with intelligent and inquisitive people who voiced their ideas.

I also joined a sorority, almost an extension of being in Modesto. In a sorority, you practice traditions together through a variety of activities. One of the men I dated was in a fraternity, so I became a fraternity sister of that group. There were a lot of frat parties where we'd dance and have great conversations. Sorority life felt like my Rainbow Girls days—being tamed because of others' expectations and feeling other people were trying to control me. On the positive side, I gained meaningful friendships and had fun participating in a variety of activities.

After graduating from college, I wanted to reach out and explore. Instead of going home for the summer, I went to Lake Tahoe and became a waitress, which was a big step for me. I became friends with many women, and we all lived together. This is when I really broke out of the conservative and predictable box, more untamable than ever before because I was more comfortable and confident in making big decisions, though I would continue to ask my parents for their opinions and recommendations well into their late nineties. I also met people from different places, not only college students, with unique ideas.

Following my move to Lake Tahoe, my parents came to visit and did a whole song and dance about how they would support me if I went back to college for my master's degree. I didn't tell them I had already been accepted into a master's program at California State University in San Diego. I applied because their well-known speech and language program offered a clinical experience with speech, hearing, and language therapy. I wasn't planning to go, but after the part about "we want you to continue your education," my parents discussed the benefits. I appreciated their explanation. Ultimately, the reasoning behind their recommendation aligned with my thinking. Seeing it as a good opportunity, I took the leap to graduate school. Before school orientation, my parents bought me a yellow Volkswagen Bug. If the Yellow Submarine and the Love Bug had a baby, that car would have been it. It was little but mighty and took me all the way from Lake Tahoe to San Diego, which was quite a trek.

The journey to confidently voicing my ideas and views to my parents reached its destination, a level aligning with my intentions to express my thoughts. It was thrilling—reciprocal conversations, open communication, and all the advantages that came with it. It was a big "free as a butterfly" step toward my untamed goal.

I have touching memories of these conversations and how they impacted my dad's ability to think outside of the box. He greatly respected and honored his commitment to our country, serving as a lieutenant in the Marine Corps during World War II. During my college days, America's involvement in the Vietnam War was challenged and protested. There were demonstrations and riots at UC Berkeley and my school, including attempts to burn the Bank of America in Goleta, our college town. The Coast Guard Reserves were stationed at UC Berkeley to protect the community during that tumultuous time, and the UCSB campus was closed, with many students returning home.

My boyfriend at that time asked my father if he would write

a letter for his approval to become a conscientious objector. They had a lively conversation, and Dad agreed to complete the necessary letter because of his explanations, reasoning, and integrity.

More than half of the twenty-seven million men eligible for the draft during the Vietnam War were deferred, exempted, or disqualified.

* * *

Since I attended two very different schools to earn my degrees in speech pathology, I learned other speech and language therapy approaches.

The speech pathology classes at UCSB were known to be highly challenging. Though not as hard as medical school, there were areas in which we had to become proficient.

Our curriculum included anatomy, physiology, oral motor, brain studies, and kinesthesiology. Back then, they posted test grades on the classroom door, listed by social security number. I remember reviewing the list and seeing that several people had failed the test.

Student teaching at public schools was also required. As students, we provided therapy at the school's clinic in a room with a two-way mirror, so the professors could observe us. The professors critiqued us while we did therapy, which was scary since we weren't yet experienced. However, by the time I finished the Master of Arts program, I was prepared to embark on my career.

I greatly admired one of my female professors. She was a gorgeous, highly professional woman who had published books on behavior modification conditioning related to and used during speech therapy sessions. I thought, *Oh, that's so cool to have accomplished so much. I want to be just like her.*

When I was in the speech program at UCSB, the focus was on naturally occurring events rather than a lesson plan for each therapy session. With some professors, the approach consisted of playing a game with a child and saying, "I think I heard a good 'r' sound," or making the sound themselves. For example, "And I heard a good 's' sound. Oh, my! This is fabulous."

But in CSU San Diego, the therapy approach was vastly different, with every response counted and added to the data collected. Let's say there was a target number of correct responses—perhaps eighty percent—to specific focus areas. We would mark every single answer with pencil and paper during our lessons. I remember being horrified in one of my master's classes by their approach to stuttering. The client wore headphones, and when they stuttered, the speech therapist would produce a loud sound to extinguish that behavior.

My exposure to different approaches was foundational to my career. I realized the headphones and loud sounds could be adapted to be more client friendly.

For example, "We're going to say our 'r' sounds now. Say this after me."

Every student is different and has so much potential. The direct approach works well for some clients, while others respond better to an indirect approach. These different experiences molded and contributed to my method of out-of-the-box thinking for diagnoses and treatment plans. It prepared me to be proficient in my therapy sessions.

After I finished my Master of Arts degree, my first job was in Del Mar, a small beach town in San Diego County, and the position was a great fit. My colleagues contributed significantly to my profession and became my friends. I felt heard and knew I was a valued team member in the school district.

My next job was in Sonoma County, Northern California's wine country. Again, I respected the superintendent I worked with who was positive and down-to-earth. In fact, I forged strong relationships with staff members, administrators, and other special education personnel.

At first, preparing for the speech therapy sessions took a lot of time because I was new and wrote lesson plans. Over time, I came to learn efficient time saving strategies for preparing lessons.

In the early years of my career, particularly at my first job, I met a lot of female teachers and other speech pathologists, and we became friends and planned activities together. There was a core group at one of the schools, and I loved meeting new pals in a new town. One day, a speech pathologist's friend suggested I go with her and his friend on a boat out to Sausalito, a city thirty minutes away, instead of going to school. She was more laid back and liberal than me with how she dressed and acted, as well as the things she discussed.

At first, I turned down the idea.

My parents said, "You don't do this. You don't play hooky from your job. This is irresponsible."

I decided to throw caution to the wind. Unleashing an untamable side of myself, I lifted my head high and agreed to go with her. I thought, *Wow. I've never done this before.*

Although there were little moments of shifting from foot to foot and stuffing my hands in my pockets because of the uneasiness I felt that day, it made me realize and think to myself, *Hey, I can do what I want if it's not affecting other people.*

Initially, I'd gotten off to a strong start with my career in Santa Rosa, but as time went on, I experienced more disappointments working in that school district. In reality, it felt as though people were controlling and not open to trying anything new. Also, I felt a lot of pressure to conform to the ideas of colleagues and superiors in the district.

A pivotal point in my untamable journey was when another speech pathologist changed how she dressed—more conservatively—to better fit in with a psychologist and the special education director. Of course, the director agreed to many things she wanted, but I chose not to play that game. I'd sometimes go to the local gym and see her there on a day she was supposed to be at school. Even though she played the role of a model employee, she wasn't.

I didn't feel comfortable telling the director about it. In addition to all of that, I was working part-time and had more students on my caseload than she did working full-time. That was the difference in treatment from administrators with personnel who played the political role.

Looking back, she was doing a disservice to her students, though she wasn't the only one. I noticed remarkable differences in special education teachers even though we all provided the same type of service. Some put so much effort into their jobs, while others did not. I shook my head in frustration as I observed those situations, but I loved my profession, and I still do. Working with the students was so rewarding to me.

My role progressed into evaluating more areas related to listening skills, attention skills, and ADHD. I loved the science end of gathering data, making assessments, analyzing those assessments, and following up with reports. Once I determined a student's or an adult's needs, I tailored certain programs toward what best suited them. My background in different behavioral approaches enabled me to treat many different disorders.

Individualized goals and accomplishments in speech therapy were foremost, and the majority of my programs were successful.

Speech and language assessment reports included extensive information on teachers' and parents' observations, as well as a review of students' academic histories. An emphasis on writing the forms in a specific way was essential in the public school setting. I felt boxed in with the requirements because my objective was to present options based on the results and to advocate for the student.

When I started there, the process was much more straightforward. It entailed evaluating a student and sending a letter home or calling the parent to give them the recommendations, which meant attending speech sessions with specific goals. That approach gave me the time and opportunity to do different activities with the students.

As time passed, the amount of paperwork increased exponentially. As a result, IEP (Individualized Education Program) forms were more detailed and much longer. They went from several pages long up to as many as twenty pages long, simply to enroll a student.

Another chief change was that early in my career, articulation skills were a primary focus of my goals, but over time, our work grew more intense and complex related to the student's academic success. In addition, our schedule differed from teachers. We had sessions with fewer students—one or two students at a time—instead of a classroom full of them. Other teachers would say, "Oh, you have it so easy."

But the reality was, we worked with somewhere around fifty students, all with different lesson plans tailored to each of them, and a speech pathologist with two-and-a-half days at one school and two-and-a-half at another. It was easy to feel like outsiders because we weren't there every day and weren't around at lunchtime to hear the other teachers discuss their students.

We also had IEP meetings with the child's general education teacher, the school principal, and the parents. We'd recommend what the student should receive for educational services and if there were related therapeutic needs such as occupational or physical therapy.

Unlike my earlier years of my career, I began to voice my recommendations frankly if I disagreed that the child did or didn't need services. That didn't make me popular with the staff, but I was fighting for the students, not simply doing what was expected of someone in my position. In fact, when it came to expectations, school principals varied in their knowledge of our role as speech pathologists.

When I'd explain my factual reasoning for recommendations, it was sometimes like talking through a closed door. As a result, it was challenging to accept not being heard and to focus instead on what I believed was best for the parents and students. On the other hand, I knew I had excellent training, education, and research-based knowledge to guide me.

It was sometimes acceptable to break out of the mold and try different research-based methodologies with students. My public school experience included various principals who were wonderful to work with and some who made my life miserable. The principal's presumptions influenced the school's limitations.

Also, while some parents fought mightily to have their children attend speech therapy classes, others didn't want their children enrolled, perhaps because they were uncomfortable with it or afraid to admit their child needed extra help.

Later in my career, I worked with severe cases and students with multiple needs, particularly those with an autism spectrum disorder. In addition, I worked at some schools with students who were nonverbal and learned how to implement therapeutic plans for them. That led me to decide that the work itself was more important than making sure I was pleasing administrators. It was necessary. I made a difference in these darling children's lives and helped their parents. That's the reason I was there. I also enjoyed practicing my skills and continued taking classes and learning the latest speech and language information and strategies.

I worked part-time because I wanted to be present with my two sons. I also kept the job for health insurance; my husband was self-employed, and because a certain percentage of my work hours in the speech therapist job were in the school district, we received medical care for our family.

Then my health coverage fee increased, so my husband and I crunched the numbers to see if the amount of money I made was worth the stress of dealing with administrators and the public school system. Leaving the public school system made sense, especially since my sons were out of high school.

Because I wasn't happy and only worked part-time, I retired at a relatively young age. However, I continued on the path of knowledge and accomplished one of my longtime goals, earning a doctorate, something for which my parents advocated. So I began my journey toward a Doctorate in Education with an emphasis on Special Education.

I strove to learn everything possible about different types of disabilities. My interest was in utilizing fresh approaches rather than only traditional ones. While writing my dissertation, other school district administrators reached out to offer substitute speech positions even though I was retired, positions that were open for different reasons (maternity leave, medical leave, jury duty). With my experience, I was confident in my ability to rapidly adapt to the processes at any school district, which expanded the diversity of my professional experience.

Looking back, I could have tweaked my doctorate to become an administrator in special education, yet this would have required additional coursework and another credential. However, as an active member of professional organizations in my field, I kept abreast of fresh ideas and advances. Diving into up-to-the-minute research propelled me to a higher level in my career. Trained for a broad variety of situations involving students on the spectrum and nonverbal students, I shared my experiences with young speech pathologists starting out in the profession.

When people showed trust and confidence in me, I soared outside of the box instead of staying closed. My outlook changed. I transformed into a tiger, striped in the colors of flame and sable. I learned how empowered and poised I could become when I'm validated.

Going to different schools also made me realize I still loved what I did and that I wanted to work part-time. In 2021, I accepted a speech-language pathologist position in a Santa Rosa school district. Finding part-time work wasn't easy, so, I was bouncing, whooping, and swirling when I got a job that fit me so well.

First, when I interviewed, the director was warm, kind, supportive, and an excellent communicator. In addition, it was a small school district with more options for my role and flexibility.

Years ago, I visualized a unique role, more viable to school districts. This role primarily focused on evaluating students, providing reports, and attending IEP meetings for special education students, which enabled me to apply my scientific knowledge while providing a vital service for children and their parents. When I was offered the job in Santa Rosa, the administrator explained that doing assessments was my responsibility.

Earlier on in my career, my intentions were to find what would make me happy in my job, and I did. I wanted to be experienced and knowledgeable and have a strong ability to apply current research to my diagnoses of students. I had intentions and visualizations. Those skills and attributes led me to my perfect job. I worked more than two days a week, but it was an incredible first year. I enjoyed it, and I valued discussing new and alternate approaches for each child.

At the time of this writing, I'm in my second year with the Santa Rosa school district. Initially, the new administration added to my responsibilities by assigning additional paperwork. As it is, I already work extra hours, so I practiced my untamable beliefs and used effective communication skills in my approach. I presented the facts of why they should not add more duties. They listened and understood. To my surprise, my request was supported—one of the first times that's happened to me in the public school system. I had planned to resign if a compromise could not be reached.

Empowering myself to be untamable strongly contributed to the accomplishments of my students and enhanced my role as a special education consultant and speech-language pathologist. Many parents complimented my evaluations as thorough and having a big impact on their child's success. I've focused on the finances of a job, but my gratification is from people.

Allow yourself to express your visions and desires. You will find you are happier and more successful. Follow what you believe in, feel comfortable stepping outside of the box, and find people who listen and communicate effectively.

Meeting My Match

To some people, being untamable means they don't want or need a partner, and that's fine. However, untamable can mean partnering with someone who wants to create an extraordinary life on the same frequency you do, rather than following some prescription for how you "should" live life. In my experience, once you've found the right person, being untamable allows you to be even more together with them. You don't need to settle for someone, even if that means waiting longer for the right person.

My road to a happy and untamable marriage was long and winding.

As a teenager, I was very wholesome and naïve. I was athletic and competed in gymnastics, track, women's baseball, and running. I was a fast runner and usually placed in long- and short-distance competitions. In high school, my early dating experiences were focused on having a good time—exploring, camping, hiking, and tennis—with guys who were into the same things.

My parents had some control over me, and Mom had her ideas about the kind of men I should date. She wanted me to date a popular man at school, interested in many activities, who was respectful, intelligent, and driven by future goals. I spent the last two years of high school dating the same person, and I felt I loved him with all my heart. Looking back, he was more like a friend. He was fun-loving, creative, and loved being an individual, and didn't conform to others' ideas. My parents loved his sense of humor, and he treated me with the highest respect. We were an outstanding couple with good values.

When I was a teenager, I was one of the "good" girls. Unfortunately, some people in high school experimented with alcohol.

My parents loved our friends, so they'd hang out at our house sometimes. We formed a reunion group (Motown) and had an annual campout trip that continues to this day.

One day, while I was on a date with David, some friends came over to my house and were chatting with my parents, when one of them said, "I saw Kristy with David, and I think he was drinking!"

My dad shot up from his chair and left to search for us.

I didn't think it was true and wouldn't have stayed out with the boy if I didn't feel safe. Regardless, my parents were uncomfortable and bristled at the scenario.

In college, I started to meet and date different men and enjoyed intelligent and intriguing men. So, even though I did not feel the need to be untamable, this was the beginning of learning to fly. I was still young, and it was more about exploring how relationships develop and what they mean to different people.

After college, I didn't want to settle down and marry whoever was available, which society and women from small towns might have pressured me into. Instead, I had several long-term relationships that lasted three or more years.

I struggled with a man who wanted to control me, which increased the time it took on the journey of my untamable behavior. When I was out with my girlfriends in Santa Rosa, he'd appear as if he was following me. Since we had many conflicting ideas, it was difficult to predict how he might behave. Therefore, my friendships with other men threatened our relationship. My flight training was a preparation to develop wings and fly.

I met the first real love of my life when I was twenty-eight years old. It was the beginning of my most formative relationship. He was eighteen years older than me. It was a May through December romance that lasted, off and on, for six years.

He had three children. His oldest, a son, was seven years younger than me and in college. His daughter was in high school, and we looked close enough in age to be friends. His youngest son was my student and anyone looking at him and me together could have easily assumed I was his mother. This is what people saw when they looked at us and tried to figure out the dynamics of what must have appeared, at a glance, to be a solid family relationship.

He was a dean and vice president of a local college. We were a compatible pair. While we were dating, I was introduced to people who were pillars of the community. As you would expect of a college dean, he encouraged me to complete my Master of Arts degree, and he attended my graduation.

He occasionally dated other women, even though we were a "couple." Once, he asked me to babysit his son while he went out. I voiced my feelings to him and declined. I learned a lot from this relationship; I really understood him. However, I couldn't accept being second-best, and I set limits.

He always returned to me, made all these promises about our relationship, and even proposed. Though we were in love and compatible, our goals were different. I decided to end the relationship.

There were a few places to go out in Santa Rosa, and one night, I was at a local bar and grill with a girlfriend. I knew the owner, and when I walked in, he introduced me to a handsome man named Jim. He had a muscular physique. I taught physical education at the local junior college, and fitness was my priority. Jim wore nice jeans and a white cashmere sweater he'd bought in Scotland on a recent trip. As we talked, he showed an interest in what I had to say, and his gaze clung to mine the whole time we spoke. It was lovely to listen to Jim's soothing voice. He listened attentively, as if his entire mind were focused only on me and what I had to say.

Jim, my girlfriend, and I left the bar and grill together to get sushi and go dancing. Unfortunately, while we were out dancing, a waitress spilled red wine all over Jim's white sweater.

From the get-go, I enjoyed his company; he respected women and believed in equal rights for women. And he worked out! Adrenaline pumped through my veins at the thought of seeing him again. I knew he was special.

On our first official date, he made me dinner at his home. Over a candlelit meal of pasta with clams, Caesar salad, and Sonoma wine, we discussed our professions and interests. He was building a new business, having recently sold a prior one.

I thought to myself, *I'm going to be with this person for a long time.*

Our relationship went off with a bang. All my friends loved him. We spent time with each other's friends. I met his brother and sister-in-law. On Fridays, we would first meet at the health club and work out together, followed by dinner in Sonoma, eating Caesar salad and mussels between sips of sparkling champagne.

We would both look forward to spending all our time together.

I remember thinking, *This is so easy and smooth, and he listens and encourages me to express myself freely.*

Speaking with Jim and being with him felt so natural. He respected me as a strong, assertive woman. I loved his intelligence, his way of communicating, and his support of my out-of-the-box thinking.

I knew I wanted to spend my life with Jim. Six months in, other men were connecting with me to date. I told him, "I want to have a relationship with you, but I'll date other people if you're not interested in a long-term commitment."

Not long after that, he proposed.

Ecstatic, I said, "Yes!"

When I called my parents to tell them Jim and I were getting married, I was almost too excited to speak. I could hear Mom and Dad's warm smiles in the bubbly tone of their voices as they congratulated me. Rejoicing at the news that Jim was becoming part of the family, they welcomed him with open arms, as I knew they would.

Before our engagement, Jim took up metaphysical science sessions, enriching his spiritual connection to the universe. We attended some sessions together before our wedding, enlightening me about meditation, mapping, and visualization. We explored having a metaphysical wedding ceremony to celebrate our love and our connection to each other. Our officiant, Erica, held a degree in psychology and was a trained practitioner of metaphysical science.

Our wedding ceremony took place at the picturesque Bodega Bay Yacht Club. Sitting right on the soft blue water, the unique building, fashioned of curves and angles, featured huge windows showcasing the Pacific Ocean's gorgeous seascape. Everyone at the ceremony could see the rolling, white-foamed waves in the background. With the lighting and reflection from the water, the room glistened with spiritual abeyance.

Erica, our officiant, sent me the protocol she'd be following before the ceremony. She instructed me, "When you walk down the aisle, glide slowly with impact, and gaze at people, so it will be a performance."

Erica wore gorgeous, soft colors for the ceremony. She said, "You both mirror each other. You two remind me so much of Jessica Tandy and Hume Cronyn—such a beautiful couple."

A harpist played our wedding song. Her graceful fingers danced with the long strings which vibrated with the most ethereal music I've ever heard.

Erica respected how we walked a path together and then diverted on our independent ways. Her speech gave our guests a deeper window into our relationship, even though they already knew us.

Then Jim placed the ring on my finger.

Erica said, "Wow! This is gorgeous!" Then she saw Jim's ring and said, "Jim, these are wings."

I loved the image of our union letting us soar to new heights, so we could be untamable together.

Even though I came from a more conservative background, this less traditional wedding was the perfect fit for me. The ceremony was far more personal and was an authentic representation of us and our love for each other. We invited a small number of guests to the wedding, around eighty, instead of the more typical 200 guests at other weddings.

My favorite part of all was when the officiant turned us around to face our loved ones. Instead of saying, "Here is Mr. and Mrs. MacNair," she said, "Here is the married couple," meaning we were equal, two souls joined in union.

After I married Jim, I realized our dynamic was similar to that of my parents. I follow my mother, a total extrovert, with a big smile.

There was a picture of my parents from our wedding, and later, Jim said, "Look at that. Your dad is quieter. He's had a strong character and loves people, but your mom was the extrovert who put herself out there more."

Our wedding song was "Have I Told You Lately" by Van Morrison. Even now, we stop, smile, and dance when we hear our music. We also said personal vows to each other during the ceremony, even though Erica shared so much.

The early years of my marriage felt blissful. I felt fortunate to be with my soulmate. I still do! I was lucky to meet and marry someone who encouraged me to be true to myself. He is respectful, romantic, and brings me so much comfort, and I know he won't judge me.

Soon after we married, Jim and I decided to start a family, but we had fertility problems. I was forty years old. We saw three different fertility specialists and went through in vitro fertilization a few times, without success.

We kept our faith that we would have a child. Our doctors were from Europe and learned from progressive fertility specialists. We intended to have babies and used our metaphysical practices and visualizations. In hindsight, that elevated my reality to a higher frequency. Frequently, I had visions of two little boy babies with big blue eyes. Finally, though it took some time, it became true!

Although we both wanted children, we endured a lot of sadness because we didn't think we'd ever be parents. We decided we would become parents regardless of our fertility problems, and we started the adoption process.

I was returning from a doctor's appointment in Berkeley one day when my doctor in Santa Rosa left a message saying, "Kristy, you need to call me. I think I have a baby for you to adopt."

Overwhelmed, I called my older sister, Donna, and said, "I don't know what to do. What if I get pregnant, and the adoption goes through, too?"

"Then you'll have two," my sister replied.

After that, our son Hunter was born. It was an open adoption, so we met his birth mother in the hospital. One of the rules of open adoption was to have therapy sessions with the prospective mother of the baby. We found so many similarities between her and us—she lived right down the road from us in our little village. She was going to name the baby Thomas Hunter, and we had decided on Hunter for his name.

When we brought Hunter home, there were so many festivities centered around this beautiful boy. He still has a relationship with his birth mother, and he looks just like her.

I was determined to form a bond with our son right away. I even learned how to nurse an adopted baby. My parents were elated and supportive; my mom said he was conceived for us.

Jim and I continued our metaphysical practices to assist with our desire to conceive a baby—visualization, mapping, meditation, and even aura therapy. Our intentions became a reality!

Although I was extremely fit and healthy, I was not pregnant and wondered why I was gaining weight and feeling tired. Finally, my doctor said, "That's because you have a newborn," even though I didn't think the same. When Hunter was six months old, I became pregnant with Cameron. So, that's how intentionality manifests in our lives.

Once we had both of our sons, it wasn't all smooth sailing. It was more like sailing on choppy but maneuverable water. For the first five years after their births, I didn't sleep through the night. People could end up start feeling psychotic running on such a low level of sleep—routinely clocking only four hours a night. Thankfully, that wasn't the case.

My lack of sleep was a state of postpartum depression. I've always been happy and positive, and this was quite a difference. Jim was incredibly supportive, and I regained my healthier sleep pattern. Once I was sleeping through the night again, I was soon back to my old self.

Hunter and Cameron couldn't be more opposite; what Hunter liked, Cameron didn't, and vice versa. Growing up, Hunter was always very verbal and outgoing, while Cameron happily played building with K'nex—designed for teenagers—when he was eight years old.

Children perceive things differently and may react to the same things in different ways. For example, if I disciplined Cameron the same as I did with Hunter, he would respond differently. On the other hand, with Cameron being more sensitive, our approach to parenting him was considerate and intuitive of his feelings. We felt we could parent him more effectively by observing his reactions.

Their dynamic could be complex as children. However, each of them, in their own way, has been untamable almost since birth and ongoing as adults.

One thing I've learned about parenting is that it's crucial to align with your partner, the other parent, because your relationship with each other is the relationship the children may model. If you and your partner are on the same frequency, the children will be as well.

We were married at what might be an older age for our

generation. I was thirty-seven years old, and Jim was thirty-six years old. I prefer to consider it the "golden age" instead of the "older age." We've been through the stages many long-term couples go through—courtship, marriage, having children, and children leaving the nest.

Now that it's just the two of us at home, we spend a lot of time together by choice. Sometimes, Jim will put on different types of music, and we'll start dancing, and he'll do a dip to tease me!

Jim and I have different kinds of intelligence but share the same frequency. In addition, we share a high level of respect, accept our differences, enjoy traveling, and have similar interests. These qualities have carried us throughout our marriage.

Jim often reads about different topics, which benefits him and me because he shares what he learns. We discuss our professions and learn from each other's experiences and, occasionally, from the experiences with my students. His comments are grounded, and he suggests different ways to approach my students, which helps even more. I appreciate that we are both untamable and think outside of the box.

Jim and I are partners on a trajectory in life, but our union has also evolved and blossomed over time, just like a flower that does not open all its petals at once. We have more together than we would ever have had apart—more happiness, better understanding, and great communication.

Even when we don't have the same views, such as particular politics or parenting differences, I'm comfortable sharing my perspective with him. I love the intellectual conversations we share. Of course, effective communication also requires specific, elegant skills and practice.

Having the right partner is conducive to genuinely expressing yourself and being accepted by that person for who you are. You need the freedom to say what you feel for comfortable communication to be realized. Your partner needs that as well. Therefore, there needs to be a mutual ability to support each other. If you have good communication, you can accept each other completely.

Being untamable is not about being wild and free; it could be. It is chiefly about being grounded in who you are and feeling free to speak from that place. When you share these qualities with your partner, you have something powerful and exhilarating—an untamable partnership.

Building an Untamable Family

Growing up, I always saw myself becoming a mother one day. Mom was so spunky, yet she carried herself with such grace. I strove to emulate that sense of humor and self-assurance I got from her. With a parental role model like that I longed to have children and emanate her gift for motherhood, even from a young age.

In her nineties, my mother said to me, "You are my special daughter because you are the one most like me."

I felt happy tears well in my eyes, a drumming in my chest, and the sun rising within me. I never felt prouder, never felt more loved, and I never felt as untamed as I did in that moment. Fluttery warmth spread into every pore of my being.

My dear mother lived a happy and productive life deep into her golden years. She passed away at the age of ninety-five and is fondly remembered and deeply missed every single day.

Before we were even married, Jim and I knew building a family was a significant part of our shared purpose. When our children arrived, I wanted to give all of myself to both of them, even though that was impossible. Beginning a family with two children a mere fifteen months apart in age was a challenge. I remember changing Cameron's diapers while Hunter simultaneously climbed up my leg. But I welcomed parenting with the positive affirmation of, *I'm confident, and I can deal with this.*

I was all-in with being a mom; it brought me so much happiness. My sons were my priority, and my goal was to be involved in their education and activities through their high school years. As my parents did for my sisters and me, as well as my friends, I loved hosting the boys' friends at our house. Hunter acted in all the plays at school, and Cameron handled the stage design and sound. We held all the cast parties at our house in a beautiful room that seemed like a fishbowl, with windows all the way around. It was specifically constructed for hosting parties. The boys' friends would come over, roll up the carpet, and move the furniture into another room to clear a space to dance. It fed my soul for the kids to enjoy themselves and bond with their friends. I knew that's where I belonged.

As much as I longed to be untamable myself, I was even more committed to helping others become untamable, especially my children, Cameron and Hunter. So, although I was an involved mom, my views on parenting weren't all that traditional. For example, my mother used Dr. Spock as her child-rearing reference while raising us. I followed some of his advice, but my go-to source was Dr. T. Berry Brazelton, also a world-renowned pediatrician. However, Brazelton's more diverse parenting approach focused on increasing awareness of a child's behaviors to adapt appropriate caregiving strategies, so kids and parents can bond more. I found that his more modern and practical approach increased effective communication between the parent and child. His book, *Infants and Mothers: Differences in Development*, published in July of 1983, was the first childcare book I read and followed.

Pediatricians T. Berry Brazelton and Joshua Sparrow saw discipline as a parent's gift to a child. Following their unique approach, which emphasizes teaching over punishment, parents find effective solutions for common behavior problems. Additionally, I felt more confident and at ease using his methods; moreover, I experienced the joy of raising children who learned to discipline themselves.

His vital advice covered six stages of discipline, the power of consequences, ways to encourage moral development and empathy, dealing with misbehavior (from biting and fighting to cheating, lying, and using foul language), and how to face special disciplinary challenges.

Parenting is a huge challenge. You need to be flexible and willing to learn. No matter what approach you take, parenting is ultimately an experiment. Being too strict is like trying to tame a child rather than allowing them to flourish and learn from their experiences. One practice I particularly liked to use with my kids was suggesting they replace words.

From birth, Hunter was untamable right out of the gate.

When he was a baby, our part-time nanny said, "You know what? I've never seen a little kid walk backward for their first steps."

He always did things in a unique way since he was so creative and intelligent. Hunter taught himself how to read letters in the store when he was only thirteen months old, and he sang nursery rhymes when he was fifteen months old. He had varied interests. Primarily, he loved to imitate people's acting while watching videos and movies. Hunter was always the gregarious child. We'd go to the gym together, and he'd play in the junior club while I worked out, and afterward, we'd run errands. He was easy that way. But Hunter also demanded more attention, so Cameron sometimes took a backseat to him.

Cameron was happy to be in his room doing creative things, so I played board games and marbles with him. Cameron would say, "Mom, you're really good for a girl!"

Like all families, ours has experienced some challenges over the years. We had our family home in Glen Ellen and a condominium in San Diego. For about five years during the kids' teenage years, we flew back and forth between the two houses.

Cameron became depressed while he was in high school. When we'd arrive home, we'd asked him why he felt so hopeless. We tried to find support for Cameron, even though he refused the idea. It was devastating for Jim and me to see our son struggle like that.

Jim and I researched a private Catholic school that would better fit Hunter and Cameron's different learning styles. Unfortunately, the first one we chose differed from what we had initially envisioned. The owners claimed they were teaching a more naturalistic approach and accepting different learning styles, which proved to be untrue.

The school was very rigid and expected their students to perform according to their standards and non-individualized teaching approaches. They did not follow the status quo—they taught techniques but taught them to learn by working in the garden, by feeding the geese, and by splashing around in their galoshes. In addition, other parents reported the teachers were verbally abusive. Other parents told us a teacher hid our son's shoes and told him to go get them.

Our children were intelligent, creative, and learning to think outside of the box, so that school was not a good fit. We pulled both boys out of that school and enrolled them in a private Catholic school in Sonoma, which taught students with unique learning styles. Their approach was that all children should be appropriately challenged—academically, socially, and spiritually. Their goal for students was to become critical thinkers, strong and effective communicators, and problem-solvers able to articulate their ideas clearly.

Although we experienced these struggles with our kids, we had many triumphs with them, too. Hunter brought a creative flair to everything he did.

For one talent show at school, he said, "I'm going to be a doggy psychiatrist." He wore a little white lab coat and a pair of brightly colored glasses.

We borrowed a poster from our vet, captioned, "How are you feeling today?" It showed different emotions. We enlarged it, then went to our friends' houses and took pictures of their dogs. When it came time for the talent show, Hunter brought out his props and spoke with a German accent similar to the famous psychiatrist, Dr. Carl Jung. Hunter did not rehearse. He performed it completely improvised. The students and adults thought it was hilarious, and he received a standing ovation. That was Hunter being untamed and successfully doing what he wanted, which continues to this day.

When Hunter was only four years old, he one day proclaimed, "I am going to live in New York and become an actor."

His intention at such a young age inevitably became his reality. He continued his journey and attended the Academy of Dramatic Arts in New York and The Bristol Old Vic in England. Hunter performed Shakespeare and in other plays in New York and San Francisco until he became interested in producing commercials, events, and, hopefully, movies.

One of our main goals was that Cameron and Hunter be able to navigate their lives with the confidence and intention of their visions and transform them into reality. We provided opportunities, experiences, and support for their passions in life.

Toward the end of high school, Cameron met with a college

advisor who recommended a sound technology program based on his interests and goal assessments, though he chose to wait. In developing his visions, Cameron researched a school in the Emeryville area called Ex'pression College, which specializes in sound arts and digital visual media. He received a Bachelor of Applied Science degree to become a sound arts engineer. It was so rewarding to go to his graduation and know he was developing this aspiration for his life.

Later, Cameron obtained his Master of Arts in Music Composition for the Performing Arts in Edinburgh, Scotland. We went to Edinburgh to see his final production and performance. Continuing with his unique talent and untamable strength of character, he came onstage, sat at the grand piano, and began producing "sounds." He lifted the top and started playing the strings with drumsticks!

Our family has always had interests in the cultural arts, and our sons are artists. We all express our untamable nature in our own ways. An untamable spirit doesn't have to mean "wild"; it's more about being free to truly express who you are.

My advice for parents and families is to be open to all parenting styles. Rather than being a helicopter parent or a totally hands-off parent, look for ways you can give your children structure and security while still being flexible. Further, if you have more than one child, approach each one differently, based on personality and needs.

I'm a proponent of being prepared, so I recommend reading books about different parenting approaches and discussing them with other parents and child development experts. Be aware that you have different ways to create the kind of family and reality you want versus passing on whatever you experienced growing up. This awareness means you're making a conscious choice as to how you parent and how your family operates.

My professional training heightened my awareness of the different ways of talking with children and how it can affect them. As I mentioned, my undergraduate education was more open and flexible, whereas the master's program was more clinical.

Being untamable is a gift you can share with your children and your partner. When you encourage them to be true to themselves instead of following prescriptions for how they are supposed to be, they will be more successful and happier than they, and you, may think is possible.

Being a Woman

~⊱✦⊰~

The 1998 movie *Pleasantville* reminds me of how I was raised. In the film, two modern-day teenagers wind up trapped in a sitcom about the 1950s, living in a small town with seemingly perfect residents. As in the movie, Modesto was full of happy families in the 1950s and 1960s, and most people followed a specific prescription for life. The mothers kept well-run households, so the home was clean, the clothes were ironed, and dinner was on the table.

The roles of men and women were very definitive. I didn't see anything wrong with the concept, since it was my own childhood experience.

My mother fulfilled her traditional role as a homemaker, wife, and mother. But looking back, I also realize that my mom showed strong and independent traits. This didn't bother my dad; he was in love with her and accepted her for who she was. As time went on, her confidence and independence increased.

When my sisters and I became older, our mom decided to work outside the home. In the early 1960s, she became a supervisor at an office with around one hundred employees. To see her as a leader, with both men and women working under her, was a formative experience for me. My mom's example made me think, *I can also do this as a woman.*

When I was in high school and involved in athletics, I began to see that many women could compete against each other well, even though they didn't play sports against men.

My true awakening to what women (including me) were capable of occurred as I was attending college in Santa Barbara. At that time, writers and activists like Gloria Steinem and Betty Friedan were making history, declaring that women deserved equal pay, equal rights, and more personal freedoms. The Santa Barbara campus was full of strong, intelligent women who communicated their thoughts in class.

It was exhilarating to observe more women having their opinions heard, compared to the insular world I'd experienced growing up in Modesto. It inspired me to learn more effective ways to clearly communicate with others.

Back when I transitioned from college to working in the public school system, most principals were male. Fortunately, that is shifting now, and more women hold leadership positions. The superintendent and other administrators in our school district are women, so the gender gap has decreased. Also, the gender pay gap was much larger then.

Unfortunately, the pay gap hasn't completely closed. Huge numbers of women still work in lower-paying industries, such as retail, childcare, and food services. Also, Forbes calculated that, in 2018, female film stars were paid thirty cents on the dollar compared to their male costars. The Bureau of Labor Statistics reported that in 2020, women earned eighty-two cents for every dollar a man earned. However, back when I began my career, it was much worse, and the public school system was discriminatory toward women, even though we made up most of the workforce.

The special education department held to a strict structure that involved a lack of thinking outside of the box. Granted, it was necessary to comply with the laws that guided us to state information accurately and to use specific forms. But we could be creative within those guidelines and still develop the right goals for each student. My goals for the students were to be functional, successful, and able to contribute to the world. While the public school system was also trying to accomplish that, the structure they used often needed to be expanded to meet the desired needs for the students, which was always my primary focus.

I remember conflicting with some of the men, and a few times with women, because I wrote more comprehensively about the students than the template dictated. Over and over again, I was told things like, "If you write this special education IEP, follow the template exactly as we've been doing it," and, "I want you to shorten your reports," or, "No, we can't see that kid that much because we don't have the time."

There were times authority figures limited me from stating my professional opinions about what would be best for the family and the student, despite my experience and credentials. That being said, I've also worked with men who complimented my work ethic and results. This was how I operated in each school district; they all responded differently, depending on who was in charge.

As I gained more traction in my career, I realized I could mobilize my creativity, education, experiences, and opinions to help students and their families in powerful ways.

The female superintendent I worked for encouraged me to be comprehensive in my job because my reports provided more options for each student. She said, "Dr. Kristy, I like it when your name is on reports and IEPs."

She gave me the confidence to follow my instincts and be an out-of-the-box thinker. In addition, she permitted me to be untamable in my job. She was an inspiring individual—a smart, brilliant conversationalist and an all-around beautiful person.

In my work, I strove to respect and connect with my students' parents. I frequently checked with them during meetings, asking if they understood what I was saying and if they had questions.

* * *

It uplifts everyone when women encourage each other to be their best and reach their highest potential. For this to happen, it's vital we don't accept the scarcity mindset that there's only a small amount of room for women at the top, and they have to compete against each other to get there. That defeatist thinking will only get in your way. Instead, shifting to the abundance mindset will move you forward and up the ladder. Let's also take a moment to define success—being your fullest self is a success. Everything else follows. Contributing all your gifts and intelligence is a success.

I've always striven to increase my knowledge and expertise, regardless of what others think. Completing my doctoral degree was another empowering experience.

I had my Master of Arts degree and was busy working part-time and raising our sons. Once they graduated from high school, I told Jim, "It's time I begin working on my doctorate."

He was supportive, although others sometimes asked, "Why are you doing that at this stage?"

I always responded, "Well, I'm tired of being another pretty face."

I loved getting my doctorate; Jim and I would go on trips and do coursework while we traveled. "Just a minute, honey. We'll go on that walk," I'd say to him while I finished my test or a paper.

Once I defended my dissertation, I was proud to put the word "Doctor" in front of my name. I've had various reactions to my title. The first school I worked for after obtaining my doctorate was in a lower-income area. I asked the special day class teacher if I should go by "Doctor," but she said the parents might not understand. "They'll think their kid needs to go to a doctor," she explained. However, at all the schools I worked for after that, I was called Dr. Singer.

My line of work is about helping people communicate effectively, which is incredibly powerful. I had a principal who was apprehensive about speaking to a parent. We did a role-playing exercise with her as if she were the parent and ran through different scenarios until she was comfortable expressing herself.

Observing people's interactions with others and their missed opportunities to engage in a reciprocal conversation triggers my desire to teach these skills. Also, I question if they had role models earlier in life.

I had role models who demonstrated effective communication. They were also committed to accepting others the way they were and perhaps were ahead of their time. There shouldn't be a discrimination standard for anyone. Whether it be in life, business, or education, we should open up, listen to people, and collaborate with them. We should receive other people and celebrate them. Women face enough discrimination as it is without other women bringing them down.

* * *

Feeling empowered as a woman is crucial. Since I was in my twenties, I've had my challenges with sexual harassment and advances from men. I was almost embarrassed to include these events, but it's imperative I share them. They occurred when women were blamed, or they thought it was their fault, prior to the #MeToo movement.

While writing my thesis for my Master of Arts degree, a principal with a PhD offered to advise me on it. Later in the session, he made unwelcome advances, rubbing my arm and commenting on personal things. I immediately left, but I still had to work with him for the remainder of the school year.

In my second year as a speech-language pathologist, the principal at the school asked me many other inappropriate questions, such as, "Where did you lose your virginity—in the back of a car or where?"

Once, I received a call from my personal doctor at school, and the same principal asked, "Are you with child?" On another occasion, after seeing this principal at a local restaurant, he quipped, "Were you with your sugar daddy?"

Eventually, he began to criticize my work, even though it was unwarranted.

Years ago, at an event with my husband, a man followed me around making advances, even after I told him to stop. My husband confronted the man, so he finally stopped following me. This is an example of a man disrespecting my voice for being a woman. How degrading it was that it took another male to defend me and stop the man's behavior.

I'm a petite woman. I took self-defense classes and learned

strategies to protect myself from unwanted advances. I carried Mace with me when it was legal, and now I have pepper spray.

* * *

Men need women to be in their full power and go beyond their fear of them. Also, they need women to go toe to toe with their highest, untamable intelligence. It's not so much about fitting a woman into man's preexisting man's but about working together to create a new reality where everyone can equally contribute their best selves.

Society has, historically, failed to take advantage of all sorts of gifts and innovations women could have brought to the collective if they had been untamed and not put into boxes. Frankly, those lost opportunities could have been worth trillions of dollars.

In the future, I'd like the reality to be that men and women are treated the same, that a woman going in for a job interview can count on being treated equally to the men applying for the position.

Keeping anyone boxed in won't help society. All our contributions are needed if we want to make the world a better place, and women need to be untamable.

Embracing an untamable state is all about acceptance, including self-acceptance. Self-acceptance allows you to accept other people the way they are. The more empowered someone feels, the more others will try to shame them, particularly with women. But being untamable involves going beyond other people's judgments, knowing that expressing yourself holds a deeper purpose than listening to that resistance. Listening to that shame shuts you down and puts you back in the box.

People can learn to be untamable. It simply takes practice and courage. First, it is necessary to be willing to trust yourself and take a chance to become more powerful because the likelihood of you succeeding could be fifty-fifty. Also, practice taking chances because it makes possibilities more accessible over time and trains you to see more opportunities for being "outside of the box." In addition, you need to look inside, realize what you genuinely want to accomplish, and be open to making those changes.

Pay attention. Observe what's happening in the world, including marginalization and discrimination. See what you can do to improve your life and improve others. In my experience, support from someone who respects your view, even if they don't necessarily agree with you, is critical.

Being unique is okay. Sometimes, your individuality is precisely what you're supposed to add to the equation. Your knowledge, experience, and viewpoints should be digested and considered. Standing up for yourself helps other people. It helps them understand more about you and your needs.

The Power of Communication

The art of communication holds exhilarating power. The difference between things that can happen when we communicate effectively and things that can't happen when we don't is mindboggling.

Although I practiced communication throughout my entire life, it was in high school when I realized I could have a career related to it. I wanted to work with children because I loved them, and still do, so much. At the time, teaching was a prevalent career for women. As I mentioned before, I had a fateful conversation with the superintendent of schools in Modesto at the end of my high school career. My mom introduced me to him, and I told him I was interested in becoming a teacher.

He said, "I have an idea for you. We have a lot of teachers already, so take a look at specializing."

I thought about how I liked to talk with people and wanted to help them. Plus, speech therapy intrigued me because it's not all about behavior; it also focuses on data. There are measurable scientific results.

As I started to learn more about speech therapy, I became interested in the scientific field. Some of my coursework included cognition, neuroanatomy, physiology, phonology, audiology, the oral motor system, linguistics and language, and the brain. The most compelling to me were brain studies and research methods in communication sciences and disorders.

When I started my career, the speech pathology profession focused on how kids sounded and helped them improve their errors. It involved helping students with articulation, voice, stuttering, or fluency problems and kids who struggled with "r," "s," "th," and other sounds.

As time went on, there was a greater collective awareness of reading difficulties. Although that wasn't the same field, it overlapped with speech pathology because the children needed to hear the differences between sounds in order to learn to read. Because of that overlap, I began to help students with issues like dyslexia and phonological difficulties.

From there, the field evolved to encompass processing disorders. Those disorders were manifested in students who needed help to process, remember, and repeat information, as well as those who had trouble answering questions. More recently, I have been working with students diagnosed with autism spectrum disorder (ASD). I learned extensive programs for working with special day class (SDC) students, some of whom were nonverbal. The SDC students have more severe needs, which requires them to be in SDC all day. It is a full-inclusion classroom setting that has a limited amount of students.

Over the years, I've loved working with so many wonderful people to help them communicate more effectively, both in speech therapy and in more extensive special education settings. The treatment plans depended on many factors, including the client's level of disability, their verbal communication, and how their issues interfered with their academic and social life.

One student who particularly stands out is a boy who was completely nonverbal. During my time working with him, I used a program, based on my dissertation, called Picture Exchange Communication System (PECS). PECS is a unique alternative and augmentative communication system developed in the United States in 1985 by Dr. Andy Bondy, Lori Frost, MS in Speech Pathology—innovative speech pathologists—and leaders in autism and applied behavior analysis. PECS was first implemented with preschool students diagnosed with autism. Since then, thousands of people of all ages with various cognitive, physical, and communication challenges have successfully implemented PECS worldwide. It teaches language on a hierarchy using pictures, starting with words, then moving to the complexity of one sentence then a few sentences, having students point to pictures to answer questions and comment.

I gave this boy a custom-made book with pictures grouped into different categories—a page with food groups, another with toys he liked, one with activities, and so on.

I'd ask, "What would you like to do today?"

He would maybe point to the picture for "play dominoes."

We communicated with pictures, but the directions were presented verbally as well. It was a marvel how successfully he communicated with PECS.

Another nonverbal student of mine was skilled visually and a whiz at spelling words very quickly. Instead of PECS, I used a similar program with iPads. His progress and ability to successfully communicate with others amazed me. He simply typed in anything he wanted to say or ask, such as, "Am I almost done?"

I'm so grateful to Steve Jobs for creating the iPad. Speech therapists now have all kinds of applications available to help severely disabled students.

I was inspired to write my dissertation on PECS by using it with a nonverbal student, mostly on the autism spectrum. However, it was just as helpful to numerous students with Down syndrome. Although the kids with Down Syndrome could speak somewhat, their speech wasn't clear enough for others to understand what they were saying. I often thought about how hard it would be to go through life without being able to communicate with some type of verbal speech.

As you can imagine, you could easily boil over with frustration from time to time if you were unable to express your feelings verbally. That feeling of an explosion—needing to release everything you're holding inside—happened to those students, also. They might have sometimes hit someone, screamed, or thrown a fit, having no other way to vent or communicate. People who can't speak have the same emotions and need to express themselves as people who can speak. I can't express in words how rewarding it was to find ways for them to meet that basic need—the freedom and the human right of communicating with others.

With my background and experience in speech-language pathology, my focus was on enhancing communication skills for these children, so I wrote my dissertation on PECS. The dissertation involved interviewing special education teachers on their successes using PECS with their students. After I'd written a summary showing several findings, I concluded that when consistently using the exact specifications of the program, I concluded that when consistently using the exact specifications of the program, the students were able to communicate more effectively utilizing the pictures exchange program.

Social language and communication are speech-language pathologies we call "pragmatics," or difficulty communicating socially. Since the COVID-19 pandemic restricted people, isolating them in their homes, the lack of exchange of information between people impacted students. Screen time only exacerbated this issue because many students were on iPads or other devices, texting and playing games when they usually would have been talking with other people face to face. This screen time also likely impacted their relationships with their parents.

Social interaction is crucial for people to learn how to meet their own needs and wishes, particularly if they have difficulty communicating. They must be able to express their feelings, another area of interaction that wasn't continually developed during the pandemic. Once we reached the slightly post-pandemic or endemic phase, many students needed to learn how to verbally engage and communicate effectively due to the lack of it during the pandemic.

Due to my vast experience, I utilized many approaches in working with students. I gained experience with students from all socioeconomic backgrounds and attained proficiency in working with a wide range of disorders, including autism, hearing loss, voice problems like stuttering, and other disabilities that impacted communication and reading.

My approach to a particular client first depended on their diagnosis. Then, I explored each individual student's learning style. I called it "reading a person." I explored things including their body language and expressions, tone of voice, and proximity. It was essential to understand the impact of these factors because a high percentage of our communication skills are nonverbal. Next, depending on their needs, goals could include greetings, initiating a conversation, maintaining a conversation, and communicating farewells. It was a hierarchy of needs, depending on students' current skills.

Not long ago, I was testing a middle school student who was a friendly boy and a brilliant student. He would sometimes engage inappropriately with other students, touching them on the shoulder and bothering them. In addition, he presented issues with miscommunication, particularly between himself and another student, which could almost escalate to a physical fight. This was especially harried, considering he was an adolescent, not a younger child. Nevertheless, he received program services, including pragmatic language skills, counseling, and a behavior plan. His speech and language therapy included viewing videos of adolescents interacting, analyzing pictured social scenarios, and role-playing.

I've worked with students across all age ranges. As a speech pathologist for a school district, you're placed in elementary, middle, and high schools, not just one level. Earlier in my career, I thought I'd prefer working with age levels other than high school, so I was pleased to teach a speech program for delightful preschoolers.

To my surprise, when placed at a high school, I enjoyed it just as much, but in a different way. The challenge was students who only progressed minimally. The therapy sessions were provided through Zoom (video) during the pandemic restrictions. I learned from those experiences and altered my approach. Working with students at the adolescent level is more about developing a solid, respectful friendship with the students to help them communicate. Communication is more complex at an adolescent age than it is for younger children. Elementary-aged kids are still my favorite group to work with.

I also helped students with articulation, which means how they say their letter sounds like "r" or "s". Difficulty with "s" is often called a lisp. Some students had grammatical problems, such as difficulty using pronouns. I taught articulation or grammatical skills with particular programs at hierarchical levels.

Communication is tied to intentionality—correctly stating your intentions. What guided my intentionality was the specific goals for each client to meet and recording the data to track progress and success. I was always positive with my students. I'd say, "You can do this! Good job!" in an encouraging tone with a broad smile on my face.

It went a long way in helping the students gain confidence and, in turn, meet those goals and intentions. Even if they didn't use the word intention, it was clear what the intention was to the students.

The length of time working with students depended on their individual needs and progress. Depending on the disability, I'd work with students for either a few years or ongoing for many years because of their many communication needs, particularly with severe students. I completed annual progress summaries for the teachers and parents to inform them of the child's progress and progression. I'd include items such as, "This is the goal they met, so now we're going to move on to this more complex goal."

My career has taught me that students' communication challenges sometimes mirror their parents', even if the student isn't aware. The parents may have communicated ineffectively, saying, "Don't do that." Instead, they could have communicated effectively, saying, "I want you to do this," which could have changed the mood and the intentionality of communication with their child. The change in wording could have flipped it from a negative to a practical, positive approach.

Communication challenges applied to more than those with special needs or children. Reading people's communication styles was fascinating. I practiced by watching people engage and observing their body language, tone of voice, and expressions. When I communicated with other adults or in my social life, I checked in with them to see if they were confused by something said or had a distaste for the topic of conversation.

The truth is everyone could benefit from learning to communicate effectively. Communication skills include social language and conversational skills. There are many resources with steps to help improve your communication skills.

Ask yourself, "Have you ever felt unheard? Has the listener ever drifted off? Has your listener become defensive of other emotional responses? Do you feel your listener has formed misconceptions? Are the intentions and emotions behind the information?"

In her book, *How to Communicate Effectively and Get Results*, Anne Bachrach outlines effective communication in six doable steps.

1. Establish trust
2. Speak clearly and concisely
3. Recognize problems in communication
4. Learn how to use tone and body language
5. Never make assumptions
6. Recognize communication issues caused by technology

One of the keys to improving communication is knowing and listening to yourself. When you know what you stand for and what's important to you, communication with others is easier and more effective. Use the positive approach: "You can positively do this," instead of, "You could do this." Make sure other people know you're listening to them by displaying appropriate body language. Show you are open and friendly by smiling, keeping your arms down instead of crossed, and maintaining eye contact.

An easy way to make a conscious effort to practice basic communication skills is by following the steps from Jane Collingwood's five steps to healthy (and effective) communication:

1. Listening: being an active listener, asking questions, asking for clarifications and perspectives.
2. Expressing yourself: using "I" statements, reciprocal language, a back-and-forth exchange, asking questions and clarifications, and making comments.
3. Interpreting body language: observation of matching verbal with nonverbal language.
4. Being aware of your differences: cultural, socioeconomics, discrimination of gender, and race.
5. Resolving conflict: interpreting the messages heard.

People are imperfect communicators, some more so than others, but communicating well is something all of us can achieve in our own way. I used different methods to practice and teach effective communication. I call this elegant communication because it has poise and grace. It involves reading the speaker's body language, gestures, facial expressions, tone, posture, proximity, eye contact or eye gazing, and understanding what's socially appropriate in different situations while also staying within your beliefs!

If you've ever felt unheard or unseen, you could have tried to "read" your speaker to see if their verbal message matched their body language or checked to see if the listener grew defensive or had another emotional response. Misconceptions can be caused by other physical distractions, such as attire, fashion, or gender appeal. Suppose a person made comments interpreted as a racist, sexist, or prejudicial reaction, such as discrimination or devaluation against women. In that case, they might have felt their prior experiences were unequal to yours.

For dynamic social interactions, it is essential to understand the perspective of others and to adjust one's verbal and non-verbal communication, including initiating eye contact and reciprocating greetings and salutations, to help have successful interactions.

People with strong social language skills function well in interactions at work and in their personal lives, develop friendships, have good self-esteem, and respect others.

Developing effective social language skills enabled my clients to express their feelings and to be heard in a positive way, so they could build worthwhile relationships with people.

In fact, fully understanding others and being understood is so momentous to our lives that I am focusing my next book on communication skills.

Thoughts on Education

Even before my career, I relished learning. Throughout my school days, I grew and bloomed mentally, physically, emotionally, and socially under the nurturing power of education. The exhilaration of expanding my mind with knowledge and ideas and sharing all of that with others never wavered, never weakened through various educational environments and experiences throughout my career and life. I was delighted to learn and continued taking classes, seminars, and training. I thrived on researching, exploring current trends, and sharpening my skills.

I was close to my teachers when I started school as a little girl. One of my first teachers was Miss Kidd, who was what people used to refer to as a "schoolmarm," a female teacher who wasn't married. My mom told me I was Miss Kidd's pet in class.

I enjoyed lessons, books, questions, notes, and everything else about elementary school. That included recess. I thrived on socializing. Since I was athletic, I enjoyed gym classes, which began in junior high school. The competition of sports offered me another way to express myself, even though sports were separated into men's and women's then. Girls weren't allowed to play most of the sports the boys could. But I shined and basked in my athletic accomplishments, which included dance, gymnastics, and running.

My favorite subject in school was English. I loved learning about the English language, which is no surprise, given my later career. My enthusiasm for school continued in high school. Kathy and I were song leaders, which was like a cheerleader, and we performed dance cheer routines with music and pom-poms. I was also voted the basketball queen (like being prom queen but during basketball season) because I was peppy, energetic, and well-liked by the team members. During my senior year, I was voted "Best Smile." Kathy and I were both popular with large groups of friends. We also had smaller groups of friends who were more connected to us. Both of my sisters also did well in school. However, they could have shared a more enthusiastic attitude.

Going to college in Santa Barbara, the surroundings became part of my educational experience as much as the school did. Modesto has been described as a Norman Rockwell area—an idyllic, sleepy town populated with happy families. In the college environment, Santa Barbara (Goleta), in contrast, was a liberal hippie bastion during the late 1960s and early 1970s. I was enlightened, inspired, and energized by exposure to a more diverse group of people.

After graduating with my Bachelor of Arts, my social education continued when one of my girlfriends and I decided to live in Lake Tahoe and work as waitresses for the summer. Since it was a tourist area, there was even more diversity in the types of people I met.

Following my parents' advice, I made my way down to San Diego in my little yellow Volkswagen Bug just in time for school orientation.

My graduate school degree opened important avenues and opportunities for my career, views on the educational systems, and personal beliefs about thinking outside of the box and becoming untamable in most areas of life.

Nowadays, most speech-language pathologists must obtain a Master of Arts or a doctorate, but it wasn't necessary then. However, I decided to pursue my Master of Arts degree because I loved learning and wanted to gain more knowledge and experience in my profession before I started seeing clients on the job.

A person's options could include a license and speech-language pathology credentials. Usually, licensed people work in clinics or hospitals or have their own clinics. I completed both, which involved classes, clinical hours, and student teaching. Therefore, I am qualified to provide services in a school setting, and I have my master's with a license in speech pathology and audiology. Having both the license and credentials allowed me to work in different settings, which I am grateful for.

For those interested in working in speech pathology but who don't want to go through so much schooling, there's the role of a speech-language pathologist assistant, which requires only a few years of education, as opposed to seven or more. I'm working with a knowledgeable assistant who provides excellent therapy sessions with the students and completes some of the required forms for special education programs. My SLP role primarily focuses on assessments, detailed evaluations, reports, and IEP meetings with parents and required attendees (teachers, principals, and possibly occupational therapists, physical therapists, and psychologists).

The therapy of speech-language pathology impacts students academically, socially, and personally. One of the thrilling things about my field is that helping students to speak or communicate changes their whole lives. The skills we work on with them carry over to other vital aspects of their lives, such as learning to read and socializing with other kids and teachers.

It is devastating to be unable to tell anyone what you want, feel, or think. It reminds me of the title of Harlan Ellison's famous sci-fi story *I Have No Mouth, and I Must Scream.* Speech and language therapy gifts these "boxed-in" students with the tools to break open the box. The marvel of connecting and communicating with others accelerates academic success and social interactions, even acceptance and equality, which society consistently withholds from those who have no voice.

The education system has evolved since my education and career. For example, teachers and administrators must complete regulations like administering state specific tests. In addition, they conduct standardized testing every year to track students' progress, or lack thereof, things that did not exist when I was a child in school.

Question Everything

⚜

When faced with challenges in my personal and professional life, it's far better to look at the situation from different angles and keep trying other ideas instead of settling for a less-than-ideal solution.

But this approach is challenging. It can be uncomfortable for some people to follow, especially those who are used to the status quo. However, the status quo only works for some individuals. I encourage you to question everything and explore the different perspectives of a situation and interaction. This approach can lead to effective communication in most business and personal relationships.

I have always been inquisitive throughout my life. When I was little, my mom told my pediatrician that I continuously asked questions and was strong-willed.

He said, "Let her fly. She's strong-willed. Let her live to the fullest."

Since I was born, I was compelled to voice my opinions and present out-of-the-box views. This impulse manifested increasingly throughout my life. Although particular experiences and situations have been an impetus, especially with administrators who share similar creative views, the need to express my *real* self was a constant one. My untamed metamorphosis impacted me personally and professionally and made my life better. A word of caution: this takes practice and awareness of the listener's body language and nonverbal cues.

For years, I've used this inquisitive mentality in my work with students, especially when I have completed Individualized Education plans (IEPs). Qualifying for special education begins with conducting assessments, composing reports and recommendations, and completing the State of California's required forms. In addition, it's in a system called SEIS (special education records).

The report provides background information on the students, their present levels, and their academic and social functioning. It includes current grades, academic skills, developmental progress, health and medical knowledge, and the parents' input. Many different areas are covered, goals are set, and suggestions are made on how many speech-language therapy sessions the child should have and how long the sessions should be.

Once the IEP information is completed, a meeting is scheduled to review the report and make decisions about the student's special education services for the year, to which everyone must agree. The principal, parents, classroom teacher, and special education specialists are included.

Not everyone will always agree on the best course of treatment for a child. In that case, I may be brought in to provide a second opinion. It will be initiated by the director of special education and will inform me that the parents disagree with the initial findings of the speech-language pathologist's report and requested a retest with a different speech pathologist. I choose tests after thoroughly reading the background information, how the child is functioning at school, what the teacher thinks they need, and what the parents report.

This puts me in the position of having to challenge another speech-language pathologist and suggest they might be missing the target tests available to diagnose students. In one case, this became problematic because the initial pathologist was defensive. The night before the meeting, she changed the information to state the results of her testing instead of the new findings.

It's challenging when you feel your expertise is undermined, but on the other hand, it happened to me in one case during my first year in a school district. I did the initial testing, which the parents didn't agree with, and a different speech-language pathologist was brought in to retest. Rather than take it personally, I saw this as part of the end goal—to help students who were entitled to speech and language services. Another case I retested a student was simple: a child hadn't received services to articulate with "r" sounds. She had been denied a skill she needed to learn earlier in school. When the speech service was added, her life changed.

A second opinion is crucial to any aspect of life where you're faced with an important decision, especially concerning medicine. Different exposure to the same situation may provide different results. New information, new eyes, and the experiences and views of different people are all important, especially when examining complex problems.

When I developed my method for IEPs—thoroughness and thinking outside of the box by selecting different tests—I also believed in approaching the meeting with parents differently. We needed to listen closely to the parents. I took on the role as an advocate for them and the students.

When faced with the possibility of a new and complicated case, I didn't say, "My caseload's too large. I can't see them."

I've always found it imperative to set aside time to discuss different opinions to reach a team decision based on a child's total environment, both at home and at school, to consider how their communication challenges are impacting them educationally and socially.

My methods may be different in the school system, but I've found they work. Offering second opinions enhanced my skills. I've been able to assist schools with evaluating a child differently, exposing additional needs, or offering other successes for the student. I've always been that way, digging deeper. If a particular test didn't show us enough or if something else was going on with a student, I thought to myself, *What can be done?*

What can we do about this?

My analytical, inquiring mindset propelled my success in giving a diagnosis that fit with the parents and the students and provided the child with the help needed to reach full potential.

I've even had parents cry at meetings and say how thankful they are. They knew something was going on. After second opinions, parents called me and said, "Oh, I wish you could see our child now."

My role of writing IEPs and providing second opinions for children at different schools was an exception. In the school system, students were generally assigned to the speech pathologist at their school.

In my career, I've been able to tap into my intuition to help my students. I don't get stuck in the mentality of, "Well, this works for me, so it must work for you."

Some speech-language pathologists approach things this way. Some don't. We're all unique. We have different learning styles and emotional bandwidths. Naturally, I let my intuition guide me now, more so than when I was younger.

I encourage you to question and examine aspects of your life, too. Open your mind and heart, explore other possibilities, and don't box yourself in. Your intuition will help you refine your intentions and create solutions to problems. I have a higher quality of life now because keeping in tune with what feels natural has enhanced my relationships and my career.

I used to call it thinking outside the box; more accurately, being untamable means focusing on my intention and what my mind tells me. But that doesn't mean I gave myself carte blanche to say whatever I wanted.

In social situations, when something bothered me, I wouldn't address things because the setting wasn't appropriate. I thought, *Well, that's how they think. I'm not going to change them.* But when I was directly involved in a situation, I would say something in a way the person was likely to be receptive to hearing.

I know speaking up for oneself only comes naturally to some people. But I think it starts by identifying that quality in yourself, the authentic, intuitive voice that knows what you want and how you really feel. After intuition comes trust. Trusting your instincts gives you confidence in yourself. Know that your contribution is good for the world and provides a more prosperous life at a higher level for people, including yourself.

I had to put my training wheels on in the school system, not agreeing with certain things in IEP meetings and special education, especially when I was younger. I said some things in ways that were not as effective as they could have been. But it's also vital to stay true to yourself. It may sound like that's conflicting advice. However, as I've matured, I have found it's important to be open to reading people and how they respond to what you're saying. Phrase your opinion as positively as possible. Instead of harsh or strong statements, use effective communication skills to get your point across.

When stating an opinion contrary to what someone else thinks or making a comment that is difficult for them to hear, use verbiage that can smooth the conversation, such as, "Let's discuss this one-on-one," or, "Okay, let's look at the strengths and weaknesses of this and what works for everybody."

Most of all, know you are valuable. You have a unique viewpoint on the world, which is an asset. Don't give up if you feel you haven't reached your potential because of challenges in your life. Listen to your intuition to see what it is you're here to contribute to the world. Try different things to see what works to meet your goals.

Generational Upgrade

Now in my seventies, I look back at the enormous amount of change I've lived through. While some things are definitely better, other things were better in the past or at least simpler.

When I was a child, we weren't inside looking at screens every day. We played outdoors all the time, so we learned how to socialize appropriately early in life.

On the other hand, life was buttoned up. People were expected to behave in specific ways. That's how I was raised. I was conditioned to hold my feelings back to avoid conflict, partly because of the social expectations for little girls to be quiet and nice. My parents were also very kind, and that was my example of how to act around others. They were socially appropriate. They attended church and volunteered in their community. But on occasion, my mom spoke up in a way that was ahead of her time, so I embraced this spirit from her.

My dad only confronted people if necessary to help his family. He was generally an introvert. He wasn't shy, but he certainly was not as outgoing as my mom. She was highly expressive with a big personality, like me!

Except for my parents, my sisters and some other family members seemed to lack acceptance of my drive to succeed. It was unique for a girl in those days to be driven to success. I thought they didn't respect me and what I achieved. My two sisters lived in Modesto most of their lives. If they experienced meeting new people, traveling, living in different towns, and possibly obtaining higher education, they could have become more receptive to new ideas.

We've made great strides in social progress since the 1960s, such as with the Civil Rights Movement. We see evidence of a more equal society, with more diversity in high political offices and the upper management of major corporations. But one issue still lingering is inequality between men and women. Professionally, women have progressed into higher positions in school systems that were, in the past, predominantly held by men. But there is still so much progress to be made.

There are many conflicts in the world, but more people are open to a discussion of what they want to accomplish and all the variables that go along with it. Sometimes that develops into a straightforward answer or agreement and a common goal.

More people are following modern approaches to child-rearing. That's significant because your child is the ultimate product you will produce in life.

My journey to becoming more untamable expanded over time. It's what I identify with in my life and my relationships with my husband and sons. I'm relaxed and comfortable with my nature because I've come to grips with it. I understand myself, and I'm happier not being held down.

In elementary school, I didn't want to hurt people's feelings, so I didn't express anything that could have been construed as negative or hurtful. I was always happy and positive, but I found it harder as I became older to keep up that unwavering sunny disposition. I sometimes felt compelled to speak up, to oppose what someone else said, but I didn't know how to go about speaking up in the best way.

I wish I'd asked myself, "How important is this to people around me right now?"

For years, I either didn't address things or didn't address them more acceptably. I now find it more effective to engage someone with verbiage like, "Tell me what you might think about this," instead of immediately stating my opinion.

I'm able to embrace who I am, which was suppressed when I was younger. I think of myself as blossoming, with all the different blossoms impacting my professional, personal, and social life. It's like when you see the little petals falling off a rose, revealing deeper layers underneath.

Tapping into my untamable side has shaped my life in significant ways. Earlier in my career, it influenced how I handled meetings at school.

I began opening up by saying, "Let's take a look at considering this, this, and this," even though some structured people surrounded me.

My opinion was different from theirs because they were in a box, but I provided examples to help them visualize what I was talking about.

I said, "Well, now wait a minute. I've observed this student doing this."

Over the years, I built up confidence in myself and what I could contribute to my career. Also, society upgraded old-fashioned notions of women's roles in the workplace to more serious, inclusive, and equal ones.

By plugging into my true nature, I shaped my relationships over time. I was clear to men that we were equal and expressed how I felt as I wanted to know what they felt and believed. My husband and sons supported me, thinking outside of the box and presenting other opinions.

Our sons' creativity manifested in different ways. Hunter is well-read, enjoys various music and fine art genres, and studied acting at the Academy of Arts in New York and the Bristol Old Vic in Bristol, England. Hunter had the experience of performing in Shakespearean plays. He is also learning the art of film production as an assistant producer of commercials and other events filmed in San Francisco, California. So, he is in tune with where society is nowadays.

Cameron developed his out-of-the-box thinking by composing poetry and music. He was a virtual reality developer in the Bay area. Cameron attended the Ex'pression School of Digital Arts and earned a degree in audio engineering.

Our other son expresses his out-of-the-box thinking by composing poetry and music. He was a virtual reality developer in the Bay area. Cameron attended the Ex'pression School of Digital Arts and earned a degree in audio engineering. Then he studied Music Composition for the Performing Arts at the University of Edinburgh, Scotland. The program consists of students who are curious, open-minded, and adaptable. It is mainly designed for students to acquire new skills and consolidate their existing knowledge across all areas for a new degree in music.

As I mentioned before, I received positive feedback on the quality of my reports. But like I said, it's easier to accomplish this when the words are chosen carefully and delivered tactfully. I had "training wheels" for developing those conversations.

My husband and I maintained active communication with each other. We asked each other how we felt about something we'd discussed, what our intentions were, and what could come out of it. And we listened to each other. Sadly, I didn't have this experience with my two sisters, who are very different from me.

My older sister recently passed away. When Donna was married, she lived in a small town near the foothills of Angels Camp, California, which was more conservative and rigid. It was a place where people said things like, "This is what we do, and this is how it is."

Donna was a wonderful homemaker and mother, fitting the mold of a girl raised in Modesto, California. She loved to read, and we often discussed books. She discovered her creativity in music, both singing and through playing piano. Even when she moved to the Central Valley in California, where my mom and dad lived in their older years, Donna stayed in that same pattern, rarely challenging people during conflicts. My dad was similar.

Kathy also tended to be more conservative and concerned about other people's opinions of her. Even though people always compared us because of our apparent similarities, we were different as well. The vast difference was that my life was full of varied experiences, like traveling, living in many different areas, and attending three universities. Nevertheless, we shared a bond of closeness and friendship. Unfortunately, my experience of being twins is Kathy continuing to try to reel me into the role of a Modesto woman and controlling me to become more similar. Unfortunately, this behavior created conflicts between us and challenging conversations that escalated after I moved away for college.

Conflicts may occur between people who have different backgrounds, experiences, and lifestyles. However, some people can overcome these challenges by sharing their interests and intentions. Kathy and I have different personalities and styles of communication. A method is saying "I" messages and asking questions rather than, "You aren't listening," or, "You didn't hear what I said." These negative comments can create defensive feelings from the listener.

There were a lot of miscommunications between Kathy and I. Challenges occurred when Kathy told me to sit down when I was looking for someone at an event. Also, she didn't approve of my fashion choices, often telling me what kinds of clothing not to wear. That's not how people dress here. Others would not like that," she said.

My responses were, "Oh, thanks, but I dress for myself."

It's challenging when faced with resistance to be inside the box when I am accustomed to flying around with my wings. I love using fashion to express myself, but my choices are still appropriate for the setting.

However, there were glimpses of my twin expressing herself. She allowed herself to be outside of the box in creative ways. Kathy began painting about two years ago and, without formal training, became an incredible artist. She has created many types of crafts as well. For example, she created a glassed-in picture frame and a memory box with some of our mother's items. As a result, the art store wanted to hire her.

In summary, my parents encouraged us to be creative people and that manifested itself in us in different ways. Also, Jim and I exposed our sons to developing their wings and flying like butterflies, free to express themselves. They ended up attending colleges in different countries with an international student body and learning about other cultures from around the world.

I'm still making upgrades to myself all the time, but it has been encouraging to see my development evolve, along with many of the overall changes in society. The future's looking bright for young women and men to be able to develop their untamable selves.

Untamable

Even though I've grown and changed so much over the years, I know that being untamable isn't a destination. It's a journey, and I still set intentions for myself.

Socially, I want to continue my path of being open. When I attend social events and parties, I don't want to spend my time engaging in conversations with narrow-minded people. For instance, at a recent party I went to, a radiologist was talking to a friend of mine about being a medical doctor.

My friend turned to acknowledge me and said, "Here's Kristy; she has her doctorate."

He began making the kind of rude remarks men used to belittle women. Along with other insults, he said, "Oh, big deal. Just like 'Doctor' Biden, huh?"

When I was younger, I would have confronted him and expressed my untamable thoughts. In this case, I turned around and walked off.

My parents taught me elegant communication with poise and grace. I've honed that communication style over my career. It involves "reading" your speakers through awareness of their verbal and nonverbal communication, along with staying socially appropriate in different situations while being true to your own beliefs.

Overcoming communication challenges entails knowing what is effective for you and how others react. To get to that point, you must reach outside of the box and experiment with different methods to see how they impact other people. You must be alert to their reactions to what you're saying.

I was at an event talking to Donna's son and his girlfriend, both who were young and educated. They asked me what I was doing now, and I explained, "Writing a book and working with Dr. Tracy Thomas' program, The Empire Company." I began my discussion with the importance of intentions and how to use them to bring those intentions into reality. I paused for a moment and read their reactions. The girlfriend seemed to be in the same flow as me, but my nephew's body language indicated he wasn't interested.

Instead of looking at me, he was distracted by the activities in the room and seemed to drift off during the conversation.

He said, "Oh, what is this?" However, his verbalization did not match his body language. Instead of looking at me, he was distracted by the activities in the room.

So, I began asking them questions about their lives. That's when my nephew shared that his employees think his body language is confusing because it conflicts with verbal language.

Learning how people communicate will help you work with others and express your desires, needs, and views. You must be fearless, confident, and courageous to developing this socialization journey. Also, if you trust yourself, you will gain the framework for out-of-the-box thinking on different options for problem-solving.

When you trust yourself, you can tune into reality and use intuition. Start when you are in a low-stakes situation and ask, "How else can I do this? Is there another way?" As you practice communication strategies, you will develop more tactful ways of expressing these challenges and being received well.

The value of being untamable is being presented with opportunities that might not have been provided otherwise. In college, there were certain classes we were required to take, but I learned new things in them. The required classes provided opportunities to see if I did or didn't like something. So, instead of saying, "Oh, I had to take this class," I started to say, "I was able to learn more about this subject."

I want my students to accept they don't have a disability, simply a different style and way of functioning in life. Chris, The Speech Dude, has developed tests, report templates, and therapeutic goals from an approach he describes as "neurodiversity." This term is especially appropriate for students with an autism spectrum disorder. When students are viewed as diverse rather than disabled, it empowers them. I have learned so many exciting things from students with disabilities during our discussions. This population deserves to have a voice, and researchers in special education have discovered some successful strategies to give them one.

I love seeing how my work has impacted students and allowed them to lead productive lives. My husband was recently picking up prescriptions for me. The pharmacy technician noticed the name on the medication and asked Jim, "Oh, is Kristy your wife? I have to tell you a story I'll never forget about her. We were doing a lesson, and I was resistant or not quite getting it. She told me, 'Okay, let's take a chance. What do you think? Could it be this? Could it be that?'" He explained to Jim, "It opened up my mind to look further into things, not only that day, but also going forward." He was my student about thirty years ago.

Although we have specific goals to meet in speech therapy, students can be creative and have fun during our sessions when presented with out-of-the-box strategies. During evaluations, standardized tests can have difficult questions. Following the specific protocol allows you to repeat some questions, but others can't be repeated. Also, an examiner cannot tell students if their answer is right or wrong. However, positive comments like, "Great job! Oh, you know a lot about vocabulary," goes a long way in reinforcing their confidence.

You can encourage yourself in the same way when tackling difficult situations. Look within yourself and at all the possibilities that could or will occur in your life. Open up to new opportunities whether you're young or old. Believe in yourself and work on being an effective communicator, so people will be more receptive to your ideas. There are many ways of stating an opinion. Use verbiage your listeners will be more open to, and you may open up opportunities that will surprise you.

The old saying, "It's not what you say; it's how you say it," is true. Approximately seventy to eighty percent of communication is nonverbal. Be aware of your body language such as eye contact, face your speaker or listener, and watch your gestures to ensure they match what you're saying. Talk with your hands and arms open, not closed. Control the tone of your voice and the words you choose. Also, keep the conversation moving by either commenting or asking questions. Avoid "always" or "never" or "you" statements. Instead of, "You always do that to me," you can say, "I'm really feeling you do this," and explain why. Also, watch your proximity; don't stand too close or too far away from the person.

To see if a person is receiving your message, check in with them by reading their body language message or by using verbiage like, "Are you with me here? How do you feel about this? What do you think?" and, "Do you have any questions?"

Learning to remain untamable and true to myself has been a process. I've learned through different experiences and thinking in hindsight, *Wow, I could have handled that a little differently.*

None of us are perfect, and that's okay. Every interaction

allows an opportunity to improve for next time, just as every generation is another opportunity for humanity to advance toward the goal of an equitable society.

Here are some steps to help you be untamable:

1. Release your fears and rebuild your confidence.
2. Let go of what doesn't bring you fulfillment, such as certain behavior patterns.
3. Learn effective communication skills, both verbal and nonverbal.
4. Develop and sustain real and honest relationships.
5. Speak your truth.
6. Break from preconditioning and prior learned behavior.
7. Use out-of-the-box creative and intuitive thinking to transform people.

The information on communication in this book is just the tip of the iceberg. I am available to consult and conduct learning sessions on social communication and conversational skills.

Conclusion

To me, being untamable represents feeling and having a happy life. It means feeling free with my fashion choices and representations. It means being secure with myself and feeling accepted by others for who I am. It means no matter what "box" I feel like I'm being put into, I can visualize how to be out of that box, and then I can make it happen.

Writing this book has helped me reflect even more on my journey toward becoming untamable. It's also made me more untamable in the process! I feel I needed to accomplish writing not only for myself, but also for other people.

No matter where we come from or what our struggles are, all of us have at least some aspects of our lives that feel boxed in. Some people feel that way their whole lives, and they never break out of their box.

If you're struggling, you can go outside of the box by doing something about it. I know you can do it because I did it for myself, and I've helped hundreds of students do so over the years, some who had very significant challenges.

You deserve to be heard and respected. Use the communication skills strategies in this book to start expressing your untamable self in a way that will get results.

I can't wait for you to live an untamable life, too.

Historical Events That Influenced My Shaping

Prior to 1870, a few farmers settled into the area that later became my hometown of Modesto. However, the town wasn't founded until 1870 when the Central Pacific Railroad purchased a square mile of land and started selling lots.

During the mid to late 1880s, Modesto grew into a more structured city. Modestans were civic minded even back then and joined the local chapters of the Masonic Lodge, International Order of Odd Fellows, Native Sons of the Golden West, Order of the Eastern Star, Women's Christian Temperance Union, and Society of California Pioneers. Several of those organizations are still active in Modesto today.

The town put together a community baseball team in 1872, which became an (independent) minor league, the Modesto Reds, in the 1890s. Theater, dancing, and music were also popular in Modesto.

The city was incorporated on August 6, 1884. At that time, the city limits consisted of downtown and a few tracts of land.

Modesto got electric lighting in 1891 and its first sewer system in 1892. In 1940, the city built a canal system to irrigate the local crops. With the advancement of irrigated farming, Modesto's population doubled to 4,034 people in 1910.

The town continued to grow, but the 1950s was a decade of accelerated expansion and prosperity. Modesto's population doubled again. With the post-World War II baby boom, the city had to build twelve new schools in the span of seven years. But that wasn't all. Modesto developed public golf courses, baseball fields, and tennis courts. More exclusive private clubs for swimming, golfing, and tennis were opened as well.

The 1950s were also the height of the automobile culture, and cruising 10th Street in downtown Modesto was a favorite way for teenagers to spend a Saturday night. When they became hungry, they'd steer over to one of Modesto's drive-in hamburger joints where a carhop on roller skates took their order for cheeseburgers and milkshakes.

The 1960s brought the turbulent years of the Vietnam War. Between 1964 and 1973, the U.S. military drafted 2.2 million American men. This resulted in exemptions and deferments, especially for college and graduate students. Some men avoided the draft by emigrating to Canada or Sweden, becoming a conscientious objector, or enlisting in the Coast Guard or

National Guard. More than half of the twenty-seven million men eligible for the draft during the Vietnam War were deferred, exempted, or disqualified.

Many men burned their draft cards in protest. Hippies were a big part of the anti-war movement and often chanted the slogan, "Make love, not war," at protests. Some protests were peaceful, but riots broke out at UC Berkeley and UC Santa Barbara. The Bank of America in Goleta was almost burned down during the protests. The Coast Guard Reserves were called in to UC Berkeley to protect the community, and the UCSB campus had to close its doors for a while because of the protests.

The late 1960s was a time of counterculture with the hippie men wearing their hair long and growing beards, and putting aside suits for jeans, leather vests, and colorful tie-dyed shirts. Hippie girls often wore granny dresses or jeans, fringed leather, tie-dyed shirts, macrame belts, and love beads. Psychedelic drugs, LSD, marijuana, rock music, and anti-war folk songs were part of the hippie scene. Another phrase that was popular at the time was, "Do your own thing."

Many minorities and marginalized Americans organized protests to gain their civil rights. This included the Black Panthers, gay rights activist, and feminists.

Feminists were dedicated proponents of gender equality in law and in practice. The women's liberation movement protested sexism, sexist exploitation, and oppression against females. Women's liberation had an enormous impact on young adults like me who came of age in the 1960s and 1970s.

The Women's Rights Movement goes back to the nineteenth century when female activists struggled for the right to vote, the right to own property, the right to education for women, and emancipation for all enslaved African Americans. The First Women's Rights Convention in the US was held in 1848. Women known as suffragettes continued to campaign for the right to vote throughout the years of the fight for women's rights.

Some headway was made during the early twentieth century. Margaret Sanger opened the first birth control clinic in the US in 1916. Jeannette Rankin was the first woman elected to Congress in 1917. Women gained the right to vote in 1920.

A new breed of female leaders emerged in the 1960s and 1970s, such as Betty Friedan and Pauli Murray from NOW, the National Organization for Women. Gloria Steinem and Dorothy Pitman Hughes launched the feminist magazine Ms. Magazine. Groundbreaking judgments were made by the Supreme Court. Reed versus Reed found discrimination based on sex to be a violation of the Fourteenth Amendment, and *Roe v. Wade* legalized first-trimester abortions.

As the women's movement continued, it played a key role in drafting international documents such as the Universal Declaration of Human Rights and the Convention on the Elimination of all Forms of Discrimination Against Women (CEDAW) in 1979.

The 1990s ushered in the third wave of feminism, characterized by an awareness of overlapping inequality by race, class, gender, and sexual orientation. More emphasis was placed on racial issues, and the term global feminism (the status of women in other parts of the world) was born. Several nongovernmental feminist organizations were founded that focused on specific women issues, rather than claiming to represent general feminist ideals.

Acknowledgements

I'd first like to acknowledge my parents, the original driving forces in my life. They were supportive in everything I did during my life, even during my undergraduate and graduate degrees, and they attended my graduations. They encouraged me to complete my doctorate degree. As I mentioned in this book, my parents were incredible role models, including how they dealt with social situations. They were so graceful and poised in our community and volunteered so much.

Both of my parents—my mother especially—wanted my sisters and me to experience all kinds of things. We had musical instruments and dance lessons, and they took us to the local theater. Growing up, we traveled and adventured by train, airplane, and by car. These experiences exposed us to learning about different communities and cultures. My parents were ecstatic when the Gallo Center for the Arts was built in Modesto, as they previously would attend the theater further away in San Francisco and even once in New York and London. Our parents wanted us to learn about my dad's experiences and attend the Marine Corps Ball, so we could meet his retired friends from the military. They encouraged my twin Kathy and I to develop athletic skills and by example as well. In turn, we exposed our children to a variety of experiences, including travel abroad.

I'd next like to acknowledge my husband, Jim, who has always been there for me. He's always encouraged me to do what I wanted, a significant reason I became untamable. He was very supportive throughout my doctoral dissertation and throughout the entire life we've built together over our decades together.

I also want to acknowledge my sons, Hunter and Cameron, who guided me on becoming a mother. At the time I was raising them, it was more about bonding with them, being positive, providing choices, and teaching—rather than punishment—for effective solutions of behavior. Even if I didn't like some of their choices, I learned to listen to them, and we would negotiate.

In addition, I'd like to thank my sisters for putting up with my uniqueness and understanding it more over the years. Particularly, I want to acknowledge my twin sister, Kathy, for her lifelong connection and support in sickness and in health.

I want to mention Erica Knowles, my metaphysical teacher. You were such an amazing teacher and guide. I will cherish your insight, guidance, wisdom, and love that will live in my heart and soul forever. Jim and I practiced our metaphysical teaching and we grew so much in our wonderful, loving relationship.

Thank you, Erica, for your teachings, light, wisdom, compassion, strength, clarity, and love.

I would also like to thank Dr. Carroll Mjelde, who encouraged me to complete my master's degree and presented ideas to help me accomplish my goal. He offered ideas for composing my thesis. Dr. Mjelde was greatly respected within the community and as a dean at universities. He was a kind, compassionate man and role model who inspired me to become an effective communicator.

Further, I'd like to acknowledge Jody Banovich, my close friend of over fifteen years. She's an incredibly competent woman, accomplished in many areas, and intuitive. We share our thoughts and opinions honestly with each other. I appreciate the trust we have, her grounded thoughts and humor, and our inquisitiveness. We may not always agree, but we can always discuss situations.

Additionally, I'd like to thank all of my former students and the school administrators who taught me along the way. I expanded my thoughts while working with them, and they provided me opportunities to see how diverse children are, a critical ability in special education.

Finally, I want to acknowledge Dr. Rachel Valenzuela, the superintendent of the school district where I currently work. She has wonderful communication skills and presents a positive attitude. She has encouraged me to think outside of the box, applying this approach to education. When I ask her questions, she says, "They're always good questions coming from you," and, "Your reports are so comprehensive."

Bibliography

The Military Draft During the Vietnam War · Exhibit · Resistance and …. https://michiganintheworld.history.lsa.umich.edu/antivietnamwar/exhibits/show/exhibit/draft_protests/the-military-draft-during-the-

Draft evasion in the Vietnam War - Wikipedia. https://en.wikipedia.org/wiki/Draft_evasion_in_the_Vietnam_War

How the Vietnam War Empowered the Hippie Movement - HISTORY. https://www.history.com/news/vietnam-war-hippies-counter-culture

Elizabeth Montgomery - Biography - IMDb. https://www.imdb.com/name/nm0000548/bio

The Roles and Duties of Native American Women in Their Spiritual Socie …. https://www.essaysforstudent.com/American-History/The-Roles-and-Duties-of-Native-American-W omen/40033.html

Bearded Woman Happily Married After Fearing She Would Never Find True …. https://www.smalljoys.tv/beard-woman-married-15

Lesbians battled for their place in 1960s feminism. https://timeline.com/lesbians-battled-for-their-place-in-1960s-feminism-25082853be90

Explaining the Gender Wage Gap - Center for American Progress. https://www.americanprogress.org/article/explaining-the-gender-wage-gap/

The Gender Pay Gap: Why Men Earn More Than Women. https://www.listfoundation.org/the-gender-pay-gap-why-men-earn-more-than-women

PECS by Andy Bondy, PhD, and Lori Frost, MS, CCC-SLP. 1985